Sanction of S. Francis  one).

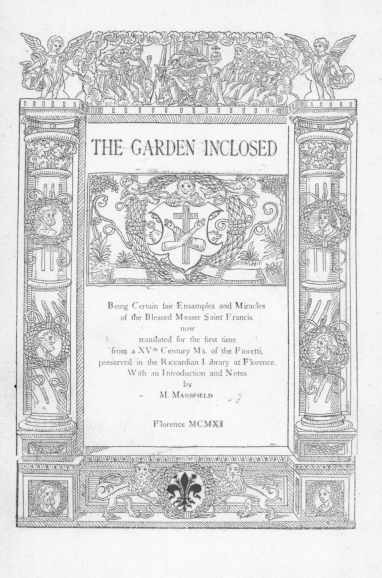

THE GARDEN INCLOSED

Being Certain fair Ensamples and Miracles
of the Blessed Messer Saint Francis.
now
translated for the first time
from a XV th Century Ms. of the Fioretti,
preserved in the Riccardian Library at Florence.
With an Introduction and Notes
by
M. MANSFIELD

Florence MCMXI

Sole Agents for the United Kingdom
THE ART & BOOK COMPANY LTD.
PUBLISHERS
28, Ashley Place - WESTMINSTER

Published by :
G. CECCHI & SON - Piazza del Duomo 15-16, Florence.
Illustrations by : Mes^{rs} ALINARI Photographers.
Printed by : SIGISMONDO BENELLI, Florence.

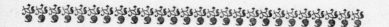

INTRODUCTION.

Cogliam la rosa in sul mattin sereno
Di questo dì che tosto il seren perde.

(TASSO, *Ger.*, *Lib.*, C. XVI, 15).

In offering indulgent readers a posy of Little Flowers which have somehow escaped the notice of worthier hands, and left to blush unseen were wasting their sweetness in the limbo of periodical literature; " truly I contrive no new thing, but have set down matters that be actually writ and are well-known upon the authority of others ".

This passage from the Antiqna Legenda, the source as will be shewn, of these little known Fioretti whose " voiceless lips are living preachers, each cup a pulpit and each leaf a book "; should form at once my justification and an apology for the attempt to glean in the field after the reapers. In that master-work of sacred Legend the Little Flowers of Saint Francis, we have the key to the spiritual life of the Middle-Ages; and these little-known Ensamples share in a great measure the sinplicity, more compelling than studied rhetoric, the poetic fancy, the graphic quality and human interest, which endow those episodes with an unusual degree of life and enable us to visualize them today with a surprisingly vivid distinctiness. Unlike the Fioretti, these Ensamples claim no more than distinguished sponsorship amid the names who earned renown in the first Century of Franciscan literature. But their present interest for us lies not so much in their literary and homiletic qualities as in their historic, I would almost add, their controversial character, which connotes the keen participation of the Brethren in the political vicissitudes of their Order. The Franciscan ideal was closely bound up with the moral and material growth of the powerful organization which exercised so far-reaching an influence upon the spiritual life of successive centuries, and called forth varied manifestations of the spirit that acted " as a little leaven that leaveneth the whole lump "; notably in the field of literature.

It is mainly through the diffusion of this Franciscan spirit that we can account for the wide-spread popularity of the Fioretti writings; and their popularity in its turn furthered the preservation under their name of much that would otherwise have perished. The Ensamples under discussion are an instance in point. An examination of the very numerous MSS. of the Fioretti dating back to the XIVth and XVth centuries which are preserved in Convent and Public Libraries in Italy, led to the discovery by the late Ct. L. Manzoni, that out of the forty-three MSS. which he was able to collate personally, no less than seven were found to contain additional Ensamples appearing there under different headings : " The Holy Mount of La Vernia, Certain noteworthy Ensamples and Miracles of the Blessed Messer Saint Francis, etc., (1). The frequent recurrence of this extraneous matter attracted the attention of professor G. Mazzoni (2) who had printed nine of these Chapters under the title of " Fioretti inediti ", collating them upon one of the seven MSS. above mentioned : i. e. the XV th century text preserved at Padua (Biblioteca del Santo, Scaff. XI, N. 22). And together with him, Manzoni and other scholars and critics of Franciscan exegesis directed their researches towards ascertaining the source of writings that appeared to be tacked on so to speak to the Fioretti, yet could not be regarded, any more than the Considerations upon the Stigmata, the Sayings and Teachings of Brother Giles, and other spiritual reading found bound up with the ancient MSS., as forming an integral part of that famous work. The Ensamples were thus traced back to the fountainhead - the Antiqua Legenda SS. Padri nostri S. Francisci et caeterum fratrum sui ordinis ; a compilation of valuable Franciscan history, tradition, and legend, now generally admitted to be virtually contemporary with the Actus Beati-Francisci et sociorum ejus, of which the well-known Fioretti are the Italian translation.

Manzoni examined only three MSS. preserved in the Vatican and S. Isidoro Libraries (3) in Rome; and his conjectures, whilst providing suggestive references in regard to the sequence of the compilation of the mass of historic fact and pious tradition that go to make up the fasti of the Founder and his first disciples, have not altogether stood the test of later research.

Publishing his conclusions so early as the years 1887-90, Manzoni undertook to issue a new and revised edition of the Fioretti collated upon the earliest known Italian text. He took exception to the version of P. Cesari (Verona, 1822) looked upon hitherto as the best, and from which most of the translations into other languages had been made, and his own choice fell upon the copy signed and dated 1396, by Amaretto Manelli preserved in the National Library at Florence (4). Manzoni had purposed to include the additional Ensamples together whith other matter in his work, but his untimely death interrupted the task when only the Amaretto Manelli portion had seen the light; (Fioretti di S. Franciescho. Loescher, Rome, 1901) and the additional Ensamples were only printed two years afterwards by Ct. G. L. Passerini in his edition of the Fioretti collated upon the Riccardian MS. described by Manzoni (5). If therefore, the alluring appellation of these Chapters — " Fioretti inediti " is nowadays a misnomer except in a general sense, and neither do they originate one and all in the Antiqua Legenda; I have yet reason to believe that they will appear, graced with the garb of novelty, before many English-speaking readers. The fourteenth century has not unfairly been called the Golden-Age of copyists, and the mediaeval hagiographers methods account sufficiently for the recurrence of the same incident in several distinct compilations. This, as Prof. Joergensen points out (op. cit. p. 110) has engendered confusion, making the task of apportionment to their authors or their first compilers, one of extreme difficulty. No attempt at such guess-work is here intended; indeed lack of competency forbids anything more than a comparison of authoritative opinions. The Ensamples taken from the Antiqua Legenda have no claim to a unique character. As is almost invariably the case in hagiography the salient incidents of a Saints life are repeated with variants in the many contemporary and posthumous tributes to his memory; and two of our Ensamples at least recur in the Legenda Maior of S. Bonaventure, and in the Treatise " De conformitate " of Fra Bartolommeo of Pisa. Regarded as a whole, they have so far however not received deserved notice (6). I would here take the opportunity to acknowledge the assistance of Mr. W. Heywood's criticism and counsel for my translation. His knowledge of mediaeval Italian is in the opinion of Italian scholars unrivalled; and I accepted gratefully the expression of his opinion that my translation would open a new source of enjoyment to lovers of Franciscan Legend. Ct. G. L. Passerini's transcript has been used in preference to that of Prof. G. Mazzoni, alike for the purity of the text and the larger number of additional Ensamples contained in the Riccardian MS. (N. 1670) of the Fioretti. The History of The Damaged Painting, and the Testimony of S. Dominic to the truth of the Porziuncula Indulgence are not found in the Padua MS. None of the other Fioretti texts described by Manzoni, offer more than eleven additional Chapters, with the exception of the Vatican Ms. (Coll. Capponiana, N. 184) which numbers thirty-seven, and this text has to the best of my knowledge not been transcribed.

The scanty information available in his day led the late distinguished scholar to follow inductive methods in his study of the primitive Franciscan writings; and Manzoni's conclusions have to some extent been superseded. The classification of Prof. Joergensen (7) which now meets with general acceptance, does not entirely bear out the theory of a single authorship for the Antiqua Legenda and a later work: the Speculum vitae B. Francisci et sociorum ejus attributed with no inherent improbability to one Frate Fabiano Ungaro who was Inquisitor-General for Hungary and Bosnia in the year 1337 (8). The latter, not to be confused with that other better known Mirror — the Speculum Perfectionis — would appear to have seen the light in the second half of the XIVth century. The absence of any record of the first MSS. text and the reference only to the edition printed at Venice in 1504, led Manzoni to the conclusion that no earlier version had been preserved. Certain passages, and the recurrence of similar dates in the Antiqua Legenda and the Speculum Vitae, and especially the statement that the writer " in imis cum essem studens in Avignone "; struck Manzoni forcibly, leading him to the opinion that the personage with whom Fr. Fabiano studied was none other than the prelate mentioned by name in the Preamble to the Legenda: Archbishop Frederic, who acts as the spiritual guide of a Friar to whom he imparts his store of early Franciscan tradition (9). The author of the Speculum Vitae S. Francisci tells us there of his pilgrimage to the Holy Mount of La Verna in 1343, and curiously enough the devout Ensample of the return to life of the Spanish Bishop, bears the same date, the proclamation of the prodigy taking place a twelvemonth afterwards in the church of Santa Croce, upon the Day of Saint Francis. Manzoni argues in support of his theory of a link: transcription from or absorption of one compilation by another; that there is nothing far-fetched in the suggestion that the Friar who took down Archbishop Frederic's words and used " his book " for the compilation of the Antiqua Legenda and the writer of the Speculum Vitae, are one and the same individual. It is a permissible hypothesis. Prof. Joergensen (op. cit., p. 104) limits himself to the assertion that the writer of the Antiqua Legenda " is a Friar from the Baltic Provinces ", and offers no alternative suggestion. Should Manzoni's proposition prove acceptable, it would allow for a period of some twenty-six years for the compilation of the two writings, an interval of time not excessive if the manifold interruptions of an active life are taken into account ; and Frate Fabiano according to his own shewing, was a great traveller.

Bearing the methods of the hagiographer in mind, it is clear that the Antiqua Legenda, and the Speculum Vitae served later writers as a mine of knowledge. Fra Bartolommeo of Pisa wove much of the material into his own work " De Conformitate "; although his indebtedness to the Antiqua Legenda judging at any rate from the very scanty and jejune account of " How the Friars came into England ", seems uncertain (10). This, is perhaps the most interesting and certainly the most dramatic of the episodes preserved in the Antiqua Legenda and the " Certain fair and noteworthy Ensamples " of the Riccardian MS. Fioretti, now offered to English-speaking readers.

The moral and political vicissitudes of the Order from the earliest times onwards, the divergence indeed commencing in their Founder's lifetime, were to weigh with century-long paralyzing effect upon the literary activity of its members. The high standard set up by Saint Francis in his Rule, was necessarily unattainable by those amongst his followers whom his powerful individuality and saintly character had alone enabled to breathe the rarefied atmosphere of perfect renouncement, singleness of mind, and selflessness wherein the ideal Minor Brother, the servant of his fellow-servants in Christ, had moved. It not to be wondered at therefore if within a brief space the dissolving force of human instinct obtained the upper hand ; and the little rift perceptible already in the Saint's lifetime widened afterwards into an impassable gulf. The elevation to the Generalship of Brother Elias of Cortona united all the forces of conservatism against what was rightly deemed a policy destructive of the Franciscan spirit ; and his fortunate deposition from office which ensued (1239) after his methods had well-nigh wrecked their Order's repute, justified the Spiritual Party as the ascetics came to be called, in their opposition. The tide of strife between the conflicting forces rose and fell according as the ascendancy of one or the other was unchallenged. Still peace there was none in the distracted counsels of the Brethren despite the attempts of successive Pontiffs, frequent as they were nugatory, to reconcile differences that had their origin in human nature and its frailty itself. These old-time manifestations of odium theologicum now are happily forgotten. The two schools of thought, for such they were notwithstanding the shortcomings of their exponents, have in reality served the cause of the Order's continuity; nevertheless they must be held in a measure answerable for the policy of prohibition which checked all individual literary expression for a considerable period.

The Chapter-General of the Order held at Narbonne in the year 1260 entrusted S. Bonaventure the Minister-General (1257-1273), with the task of compiling a new and authoritative account of their Founder's Life to replace " by an earnest and truthful " narrative in a single New Legend, the several existing Lives of S. Francis. " Ut ablata " varietate multarum legendarium ex diversis historiarum fragmentis " quae de S. Francisco circumferebantur, gravem et sinceram ipse con- " cinnaret historiam ". Joergensen justly points out (op. cit. pp. 77, et seq.) that S. Bonaventure who was born in the year 1221 had at best only a child's recollection of S. Francis, describing the miraculous healing obtained for him throught the Saint's intercession " in puerili aetate " He observes that having entered the Order at the age of seventeen, twelve years after his death, the compilation necessarily partakes of the character of a mosaic of heterogeneous material with no claim to accurate chronology. S. Bonaventure set himself to collect and weave together " as best he knew " the scattered fragments of Franciscan legend : " Actus et verba quasi fragmenta quaedam partim neglecta partimque dispersa, quamquam plene non possem, utcumque colligerem, ne morientibus his, qui cum famulo Dei convixerant, de- perirent ". The results of his labours submitted to the Chapter-Ge- neral at Pisa three years afterwards, met with the warm approval of that body; and the suppression of all the other Legends or collections of Sayings and Teachings of the Founder was resolved upon with, as time was to shew, happily ineffective severity. The Chapter-General of Paris in the year 1266 confirmed the drastic action of their pre- decessors. They laid under the ban all the Lives and Books of Sayings of S. Francis other than the " New Legend " compiled by their Gene-

ral, which was henceforth to rank as the sole and officially autho-
rized version of his life and works. The Friars were commanded
" under obedience " to suppress all those Legends, and wherever they
" should meet with them outside the Order, to destroy them ; since
" the biography compiled by the General (S. Bonaventure) had been
" gathered from the lips of those who had constantly dwelled (quasi
" semper fuerunt) with the blessed Francis, and hence wrote with a
" certain knowledge of the facts " (11). The edict was probably only
directed to the limitation of exuberant fancy, and not intended
actually to prohibit the recording of devout reminiscence of events
which at that time might still be within the personal recollection of
many " Elder Brethren ". Be this as it may, and critics, says F. Paschal
Robinson (op. cit.) are " somewhat divided as to the precise aim and
" scope of this decree.... there can be no doubts as to the effect : it
" resulted in the suppression of nearly all the primitive Franciscan
" documents " (12). The Legenda Maior of S. Bonaventure thus held
the field and gradually all the earlier writings disappeared from view,
and with the exception of the Fioretti, the later XIVth century writings
also suffered an unmerited eclipse. " As is known, writes F. Robin-
" son, it was not until the second half cf the 18th century that the
" Vita Prima (Celano) was published for the first time together with
" the traditional Legenda Trium Sociorum, and not until the begin-
" ning of the 19th, that the Vita Secunda was printed ; while his
" Tractatus De Miraculis did not appear until 1899 " (13). The Speculum Perfectionis which purported to be fragments of Brother Leo's
suppressed writings only saw the light some twelve years since in its
entirety (14).

The zeal for uniformity thus displayed by the Chapter could not
however prevent tradition being carried onwards orally or by written
word from Convent to Convent for the spiritual solace and edification
of the Brethren. That such was the case is clear from the epilo-
gue of the devout Ensample of the Spanish Bishop ; the narrative
" being writ by the Reader of Lucha to Brother Lodovico the Rea-
" der of Florence, who had learned it from.... one.... who was pre-
" sent ". Neither had the Capitular decree " per obedientiam " un-
questioned force after forty years. The Preamble to the Antiqua
Legenda (Italian text of the Vatican Library MS. Coll. Ottoboni,
N. 681) is enlightening both as to the spirit prevailing in the Order and the method of compilation followed ; the hagiographer using

his discretion in taking and leaving portions of his predecessor's
work. " Certain other matters, the writer tells us ", I took from the
" Ancient Legend " which the General in " Avignon caused to be read
" in my presence at the table to shew that it is good, true and trust-
" worthy. I have set down firstly the wondrous Acts and Miracles
" of our Father which be not writ down in the New Legend, and
" that I found in the book of the reverend father and lord Miser
" Federico the Archbishop of Rigosa of our Order. Certain other
" matters I gathered from those books written in the hand of the
" Blessed Companions of the holy Francis, and the Sayings and
" Acts of those Companions even as they have been dictated by the
" blessed Fathers. Furthermore, have I collected the Acts of the Saint-
" ed Anthony, of Brother Joanne of La Verna, and of several more
" whose memory is hallowed, and their names be set down in the
" Book of Life ".

The dawn of the XIV th century heralded better days for the Spiritual Party, coinciding with a renewed interest in their glorious past.
Portions of the suppressed writings of Brother Leo, Brother Bernardo,
Brother Masseo and other " Elder Brethren ", which had been handed
down by tradition were being diligently collected. The suggestion that
some of these Sayings and Teachings constituted the book of Archbishop Frederic has found favour; and it is now generally admitted
(cf. JOERGENSEN, op. cit., pp. 84-101) that the synopsis of the virtues
most desirable in a Minor Friar, illustrated by Ensamples of Pro-
verty, Lowliness, and Obedience under the title of Speculum Perfectionis, appeared in or about the year 1318 (15). The support extended
to the diffusion of Franciscan " Patristic writings " under the Generalship of Fra Gonzalo da Balboa, 1303-1316 was continued under his
successor Fra Michele da Cesena, 1318-3328. He it was who caused
the " Ancient Legend " to be read in the Refectory at Avignon, and
this Ancient Legend (cf. JOERGENSEN, op. cit., pp. 101-5), is none other
but the Legend of the Three Companions.

With the first half of the XIV th century the magnificent cycle of
primitive Franciscan literature closes. It offers an unrivalled manife-
station of poetic fancy in the writings of S. Francis himself; and the
history and Legend inextricably woven together, of the beautiful Legend of the Three Companions (16), the Lives of Thomas of Celano (17),
the Legenda Maior of S. Bonaventure (Legenda Nova), the Speculum
Perfectionis, the Antiqua Legenda, and last but not least the Actus

Pope Nicholas IV and the Emperor of Constantinople. (Benozzo Gozzoli).

beati Francisci or Fioretti, a monument " aere perennius " to the genius of their authors.

The almost immediate diffusion of the Fioretti in the vernacular gave them a start in popularity whereby they soon outstripped all and any other similar works either of devotion or spiritual entertainment. The Flowers of S. Gregory, S. Jerome, etc., were by common consent set aside ; and the Fioretti of S. Francis copied repeatedly in MS. and learnt by rote in every monastery of the Order increased, gathering to themselves a vast mass of miscellaneaous literature in the form of spiritual Considerations, Sayings, Teachings and Ensamples, which by this means were preserved from destruction. The somewhat remarkable fact that our additional Chapters are included in so many MS. versions of the Fioretti, varying little either in number or the episodes selected for transcription ; points to a single source, viz. the most accessible and intelligible text. Would it, I suggest with all diffidence, be possible that a Florentine MS. was used, of which our Riccardian text may be the transcript? The Art of copying flourished exceedingly in Florence, Amaretto Manelli we know was one of a distinguished dynasty. His signed and dated version of the Fioretti brings us very near to the original in point of time, and his son Francesco the first copyist of Boccaccio's " Decameron " carried on his father's calling well into the XVth century.

The invention of printing rendered the Fioretti a farther service. A first edition was issued at Milan in 1447, and the number of reprints and translations which followed in every language has been reached by no other work of devotion excepting that masterwork of spiritual guidance and teaching, the Imitation of Christ. The evil fate which befell so many of the primitive Franciscan writings may not be held altogether unaccontable for the neglect suffered by the Antiqua Legenda as a whole ; it is to accident however that we must look for the omission of our Ensamples from the first printed version of the Fioretti. A consensus of opinion has singled out Brother Ugolino da Monte S. Giorgio for the Master's degree in the Art of sacred Legend (18), and Brother Leo, Brother Giles and his trusted Companions his precursors were no less diligent workers in the " garden inclosed "; yet the unnamed disciple of Archbishop Frederic, albeit a labourer of the eleventh hour, is indeed and these Ensamples speak for themselves, well worthy of that gifted company.

I have made extensive use of Brother Thomas of Eccleston's Chronicle (in F. Cuthbert's scholarly translation) to assist conjecture — an attractive if somewhat hazardous pursuit — in respect of the identity of some of the dramatis personae in the sixth Ensample, describing " how Saint Francis " first sent the Friars to these shores. This episode, to my mind the most important of the series, is told in a few words by Eccleston without any attempt to create an atmosphere of reality in which the little band of missionaries lives and moves, such as pervades the Legend. His nomenclature however is valuable, giving us not only their names but their country of origin, and he furnishes important data concerning the growth of the Order during Brother Agnello of Pisa's short but well-filled life, and his ministrations as their first Provincial Minister in England; not to mention the circumstance that the powerful individuality of the Anglo-Saxon element soon made itself felt in the counsels of the Order, influencing their determination to uphold the Franciscan spirit of their Rule against aggression from without and internal dissension. F. Cuthbert's text and notes have proved of the utmost use to me in clearing up time-honoured misapprehensions and completing Eccleston's data. We are told the Abbot's name : John of Reading, and that of " the mighty Bishop ", Ralph of Hereford, " who carried the waterbarrel and " the stones upon their shoulders, out of lowliness for the buil ding " of the monastery " (19). Eccleston's reference to Sir Simon of Longton (Langton ?) as Archdeacon of Canterbury suggests the identity of this prelate with the Archdeacon to whom the Archbishop of Canturia addresses his memorable words, and with a namesake Simon of Langton (20) whose election to the See of York by the Chapter, was set aside by the Pope. This suggestion of identity carries with it a farther probability if it be borne in mind that the Archbishop of Canterbury at the time was Stephen Langton a brother of the firstnamed. The saying put into Archbishop Stephen's mouth therefore connotes a date prior to the year 1228, for the ordination of Brother Agnellus when the words : Let them come up, the Brethren of the Order of Apostles, were probable used for the first time. The Friars landed at Dover in 1224 and Archbishop Stephen governed the see from 1207 to 1228. Brother Agnellus who must have been a man after S. Francis's own heart is described " as a youth of amiable parts and great piety aged about XXX years ". But he must have been more than that since Eccleston's Chronicle offers us the portrait besides of a very able administrator and indefatigable fisherman of men's souls (21). The inclusion of Br. Albertus of Pisa in the little band of brothers is a mistake, as F. Cuthbert is careful to point out. The writer of the Ensamples limits himself to naming him, and one misses the personal touch so happily introduced in the case of Agnellus. For that Friar (22) who succeeded him in the Provincial Ministry of England, and the notorious Br. Elias in the Generalship of the Order upon the deposition of the latter, must have shewn no less ability in this Ministry so graphically described by Eccleston. The English Province also be it noted, furnishes his successor in the Generalship in 1240 : the able and masterful Brother Haymo.

It is clear from Eccleston's words, writing virtually as an eyewitness, (1231-1258, circa) (23), that the welcome extended to the Friars by the King, Henry III., the clergy and laity, was both friendly and generous. The regrettable breach of the laws of hospitality upon the part of a Benedictine Prior and his Monks, visited upon them all with dramatc swiftness must, if it occurred at all, have been so exceptional as to call for notice and supply a preacher with a text and its moral. It matters little however if the episode sins or not in improbability; its merit in our eyes lies in the life-like action and the literary quality of the story, the conciseness yet pictorial effect of the descriptions and the close characterization of the actors. Those poor Friars are our fellow-men and their fears appeal to us with a sense of reality. The darksome forest, " the weather being with rain most inclement " must have struck terror into the heart of the sunshine and colour-loving Italian wayfarers, in the " gloomy wood astray, gone from the path direct ". Their scurvy welcome is delightfully told, and the pictorial completeness of the trial and condign punishment meted out to the " wicked little Prior ", was certainly intended to, and doubtless justified the hopes and fears of a pious God-fearing audience. Its dramatic quality certainly conduced to the preservation of a Legend that, were a choice commanded, we would single out for preference. F. Cuthbert deplores justly " that the Chronicle of Thomas of " Eccleston is all too meagre.... his work has not the descriptive charm " of the Fioretti ". The inheritance precisely of this charm marks our compilers literary kinship with the Master of the Little Flowers, which Brother Thomas lacks ; despite his diligent and accurate enumeration of facts and dates. Our compiler is an artist of the pen, no detail however minute escapes him for the reconstruction of a scene. The perilous quest of the Friars impresses us with a haunting sense of reality in the episode of the young Monk's dream and its moral. Nor can we help feeling that home-sickness, a yearning for the sunshine of Italy, inspired the writer to add the inclemency of the British climate to the miseries of the travel-stained and foot-sore wanderers. Italian summer warmth on the other hand envelops the scene : Anno Domini MCCC.VIIJ. when the cavalcade of Messer Francesco, the nobleman from remote Apulia enters upon this homeward march. Messer Francesco has journeyed to Assisi with his train to gain the Blessed Indulgence of the Porziuncula, carrying with him a hind whose zeal is actuated more by the hope of material gain than spiritual reward. The discourse of master and man reveals the character of both as in a flash, as the latter gladly relinquishes the fruits of his pilgrimage for a " lift home " upon a pillion behind his master. The appearance of the Knight's brother in their midst " at noon-day " to return thanks for the gift that has procured his deliverance from the pains of Purgatory carries us in spirit to the little church of Rivotorto sanctified by Saint Francis' memory but a mile or so from Assisi ; where the pilgrims were wont to halt under the grim grey mass of Monte Subasio in the tree-less and sun-parched valley. Here " creation proceeding from the heat-oppressed brain ", the stoutest hearts might well see visions. The date 1308, leads us back to the Assisi of Giotto's day The decoration of the Upper Church of S. Francis was virtually complete, and Messer Francesco must have paused in wonderment before the series of " histories " that honour his Patron's life and labours. Among these it is interesting to find the episode of the wounded man whom the Saint's touch heals of his hurt ; one of the Legends selected alike by S. Bonaventure and our compiler. S. Bonaventure's version appears however to have inspired the painter, for the injured man is attended by a physician whom our Ensample does not mention, and the artist too interprets in almost humorous fashion the mixed feelings with which the " cure " evidently inspired both his wife and kinsfolk (24). Prof. Thode observes justly that Giotto excelled in the character portrayal of his actors but treated the scenery of his " histories ", whether landscape or architecture as the symbols of the strait and narrow of the way leading to Eternal Life and the splendour and glories of God's City. We must therefore look rather to the art of Benozzo Gozzoli a century and a half later for an adequate representation of the Umbrian prospect that gladdened the pilgrims sight, from Spoleto past Bevagna and Montefalco on their way to Assisi for the Indulgence of S. Maria degli Angeli. We turn to him also for our portraits. Fra Jacopo da Montefalco commissioned a series of twelve " histories " of their Founder's life for the church of S. Francesco in his native city. Brother Joanne of La Verna's thoughtful counternance figures in the medallions painted to commemorate their worthies in the apse of the church beside Saint Louis and the Latin Emperor of Constantinople, John of Brienne, This personage, whom his contemporaries compared with Judas Maccabaeus and Hector ended his days under the robe of a Minor Friar; and the manner of his call to a religious life is told in the last Ensample (25). The thrice repeated vision is described with no particular originality. The reference to the Emperor's confessor, Brother Agnello by name, carries us back to his name-sake the leader of the missionary band of Friars to England; but the period of the Emperors reign and his death (1228-37) cover that of his mission in England. We might perhaps look for this B. Agnello among the first twelve disciples of S. Francis, whose names have been preserved for us in the Legend of the Three Companions: Brother Agnolo di Tancredo.

Two Ensamples describe miracles performed by S. Francis in his lifetime, and shew him to us in his wonted capacity of the peace-maker and user of the soft answer that turneth away wrath. One only of his Brethren, Andrea of Siena, is mentioned by name. It is safe however to apprehend that he was attended on these occasions by Brother Massaeus his faithful friend and counsellor and some one or other of the Companions of his heart.

The remaining Chapters partake rather more of the nature of historical landmarks in the controversy concerning the traditional grant of the Porziuncula Indulgence to S. Francis in person by Pope Honorius III. This question which agitated Franciscan councils for close upon a century, involved also their relations with other religious Orders notably the Dominicans; whose zeal for the cure of souls would not, if our Ensamples be deemed evidence, have always been tempered by principles of brotherly love and fair dealing. S. Dominic with S. Peter Martyr appear, to testify to the validity of the Indulgence in favour of a good dame who has come all the way from Germany to gain it; whilst in the History of the Damaged Painting, the culprit is a Dominican Friar, who being touched by remorse, would rather be cast out from his Brotherhood than conceal, as he in bid for the credit of the Order, the mighty prodigy wrought in behalf of the Franciscans through his sin against Holy Humility.

In his exhaustive dissertation printed recently in the Arch. Fran. Hist. (26), P. Holzapfel, O. F. M. sets forth in detail the arguments favourable and contrary to an acceptance of the tradition. He admits all the difficulties that surround the proposition of the grant personally to S. Francis, but he would in no wise reject early evidence merely upon in the ground of most of it being hearsay. The fact of an ancient belief being held by general consent militates in its favour, and at all events he contends that the privilege itself must, in the words of Prof. Sabatier (Revue Historique, 1896), be reckoned among the historical facts which can no longer be seriously challenged. No fewer than four of our Ensamples treat of the Porziuncula Indulgence, which proves the interest displayed in the controversy throughout the XIIIth century, and afterwards also, since the compiler of the Antiqua Legenda deemed their interest to be sufficiently actual to require the inclusion of those episodes in his work. Indeed the first Chapter of the series has probably some connexion therewith.

The meeting of Pope Nicholas III, with the Minister-General and other dignitaries of the Order " coucerning the definition of their Rule " may not improblably connote an Enactment of the General at that time Fr. Bonagratia (1279-83), which forbade the Brethren to receive offerings in coin from the faithful during the Festival of Aug. 1st and 2[d], lest imputations of avarice and greed mar the fair repute of their church (27). Fr. Bonagratia would in all likelihood have desired to lay his pronouncement before the Pope who had shewn always himself their generous and staunch protector. The chronicler moreover causes him to exalt the virtue of Poverty dearest to the Founder, bidding whosoever vould be saved put on the garb of the Minor Friar. This Ensample may serve also an an illustration of the Hole See's action in regard to the strife of conflicting tendencies with in the Order, The date of the episode, 1780 " ab Incarnatione " presumably, agrees with that of the Bull " Exiit " given in the year 1279 (according to modern time reckoning) whereby the Pope endeavoured, fruitlessly as the history of the immediately succeeding years proved, to adjust the differences of the rival parties, by investing the Holy See with their patrimony. The Brethren in obedience with their vow of Poverty, retained only the usufruct of their possessions.

That stalwart fighter and good hater Dante, has pilloried Pope Nicholas III, plunging him in the fiery gulf among the simoniacs (28),
and the historian Giovanni Villani (29) is not less severe in his strictures
upon his character. The judgment of contemporaries must have due
weight in assigning his place in history to this Pontiff, but we should
not be averse to discern, with Prof. Thode (op. cit., pp. 40·51), a trace
of esteem for his memory, in the decoration the Orsini Chapel of the
Lower Ghurch at Assisi (30). Cardinal Napoleone Orsini caused the
life and Miracles of S. Nicholas of Bari to be painted to commemorate his brother the younthful Cardinal Gian-Giacomo and the
name-sake of Nicholas III. his kinsman; the work being intended
also to mark his gratitude towards Pope Nicholas IV. the Franciscan
Friar to whom he owed his elevation to the Cardinalate.

This examination of these " noteworthy Ensamples and Miracles of
Messer Saint Francis " would not be complete without a full acknow-
ledgment of the use I have made of the learned papers by PP. Robinson,
Kruitwagen, Golubovich, and Holzapfel in the Arc. Fran. Hist. (Quaracchi, 1908), Prof. Joergensen's important hife of the Saint, and Manzoni's
writings, from which the passages quoted and translated from the Antiqua Legenda and the Speculum Vitae S. Francisci have been taken.
The illustrations: photographs from paintings by Giotto, Benozzo Gozzoli, and Tiberio d'Assisi, at Assisi and Montefalco, which have a
distinct bearing upon these Ensamples are reproduced by the kind per-
mission of MM. Alinari of Florence, to whom my thanks are due.
And in conclusion I would proffer my humble posy culled in the " garden inclosed " of Saint Francis: the second bloom so to speak from
his evergreen rose-bush in the cloister of S. Maria degli Angeli ; " to
" all those — in the words of the Antiqua Legenda — into whose
" hands this book shall fall, with the hope that for this work of
" mine, a share in their deserts of holiness and brotherly love be
" vouchsafed me by my Lord Jesus Christ, to Whom be honour and
" glory ".

M. MANSFIELD

Florence, 1910.

Saint Francis. (Simone Martini).

CHAPTER I.

AN ENSAMPLE OF EXCEEDING PIETY AND HOLINESS.

NNO Domini M.CC.LXXX. Pope Nicholas III., being in his chancery with the Minister-General and certain Provincial Ministers, and conferring together concerning the definition of their Rule; a certain man clad in the garb of the Friars Minor came in to the chamber to take thence some thing, withdrawing anon. And he had but gone without when, quoth Pope Nicholas: "Saw ye that lay-brother who even now entered the chamber?" "Yea" answered those Friars. To whom Messer the Pope spake thus: I would tell you of this man's calling. When I was elected Pope I straightways bid an Abbot of the Order of Cestella (31) send me a lay-brother, — virtuous, trusty, and discreet; who might have care of my person and should serve me diligently. And he hath sent me him that ye saw but now come hither, garbed in your habit. It befell one day that marking certain Minor Friars come for their bread to our gate, he began to grieve and fell into a deep melancholy. Beholding him thus distressed, I asked the reason of his grief, and the lay-brother, seeing that I was full minded to know it, made answer: Most Holy Father, the reason of my sorrow is this; that, erstwhile a cleric of my Order I lay

one day in prayer, whether in the body or out of the body
I cannot tell (32); when methought I saw all the city
in a mighty tumult. Whereat I queried of the folk that
were running: What be this? what be this? Lo! answered
they, we go out for to see Our Lord Christ Jesu! Accordingly I likewise set forth to run with the multitude,
and reaching the market-place I found it filled with men
standing in good order in a ring; and in their midst beheld
I Our Lord Christ with the Holy Stigmata, clad in the
robe of the Friars Minor, preaching with arms outstret-
ched. And thus spake He: Verily, whosoever would save
his soul alive, let him follow Me, and put on the gar-
ment wherewith I am clothed. " Wherefore marking me
that those Friars who come for the bread be clad in the
selfsame garb that I had seen Our Lord Christ wear; grief
at once overcame me, and such is my sore bitterness,
that never shall my heart be glad nor my soul comforted,
an I see not myself vested with that habit. Now I beseech
you for the sake of His Passion, so you would have me
comforted, to clothe me with that robe. " Whereupon I
commended his own Order highly to him, to wit that it
be an ancient Order, of proved worth, virtue and holiness; yet failing with my discourse to cheer his mood,
I forthwith vested him, as ye saw but now, with your
habit. And it seemeth me his dream was and shall be the
truth, howbeit as ye know full well, whosoever would be
saved must follow Christ. Yea let them, being garbed
as Friars Minor deny the body, living in contemplation
of the Spirit, and eschew the world and the vanities
thereof.

The Saviour with SS. Francis, Nicholas of Bari and John. (Giottino).

CHAPTER II.

A DEVOUT ENSAMPLE AND MIRACLE OF SAINT FRANCIS.

N the year M.CCC.XLiij, in the kingdom of Chastella in Spain, there was a Bishop of the city of Rodi (33) named Peter; and albeit, so it pleased God, he were a sinner, withal was he a fervent votary of Saint Francis. The said Bishop having fallen sick [though] of no heavy sickness, a vision was vowchsafed to one of his servants: Lo! he saw certain black hounds issue forth from the ground and assail the Bishop who was seated upon his throne, and they rent his garments all to pieces upon his back. But a Minor Friar stepped forward from behind the throne, and checked these hounds, putting them to flight; whereupon thus spake that Friar to the servant: " Go thou and tell the Bishop to confess his sins and do penance, forasmuch as his wickedness hath given power over him to those hounds, which be demons. Awakening from sleep, the man went and related the vision in due order and privily to the Bishop. Whereat he arose in his choler exclaiming that his disorder be not such that he need have shrift. And three days passed, when the servant had another vision: to wit he beheld two great dogs black and of fearsome aspect about to fall upon the Bishop to devour him; but a Brother of the Friars Minor foiled them, driving them thence; and again spoke he to the servant: " Go thou and warn the Bishop that he confess his faults and do penance, for verily within a brief space of time shall he die of this sickness. And the servant departed and told these matters in order to the Bishop; whereat he was moved to wrath, and inveighed against the man because he had said that he should die; and no penance nor shrift did he perform. And three days elapsed and the servant had another vision. Lo! he descried a great furnace above which hung a cauldron filled with boiling pitch, and the fiends had seized the Bishop, and were about to cast him in; but that Minor Friar forbade them, and said to the servant: Go thou and admonish the Bishop, that surely he will die of his disease and he cannot be healed: let him confess his sins and not tarry. Thereto the servant made answer: In sooth I have warned him already, and by no means will he give credence to me; grant me therefore a sign whereby he shall believe and confess his faults. Quoth the Friar: dip thy finger in this pitch, and speak these words to the Bishop: Saint Francis whose votary thou art hath vouchsafed this thing to me, and in earnest of the truth of my speech, behold my finger wrapped in the pitch, the burning whereof hath withered it entirely. The servant thereupon hastened to relate what he had seen word for word to the Bishop; who, struck with amazement at the sign of the withered finger, and being moved to remorse through his devotion towards Saint Francis, straightways confessed the error of his ways. And the sickness waxing grievous upon him, within a brief space departed he this life.

But the Bishop's brethren and his kinsfolk kept his death secret three days that they might carry off his chattels together with all the belongings of the house. And upon the fourth day of the month of May, anno M.CCC.XLiij, his remains were borne to the Monastery of the Friars Minor. And the Brethen had intoned the Office for the Committal, when this Bishop sat upright on his bier in the sight of the assembled multitude. Whereupon the kinsfolk, aware that he had been dead four days already were preparing to make good their escape ; behold the Bishop lifted up his voice after them, crying aloud : flee not hence ! In very sooth I that was dead am now quick. Lo ! my soul having left the body, I was carried up for judgment before Christ our Judge, and sentence of fire everlasting was given against me upon two counts : to wit, firstly, that in the confession which I had made of keeping a concubine, I felt not true contrition ; the second being that I was minded not to put her from me, she whom I had ever kept by my side, albeit ostensibly I had cast her out. But Messer Saint Francis straightways appeared on my behalf, and pleading three counts for me before Christ our Judge, alleged firstly : the exceeding veneration I had ever manifested for his person, secondly the alms which I had always distributed to the Friars, for his sake, wherefore my house and my possessions have profited his Brethren more than mine own people ; and thirdly, the mighty faith I had evermore placed in Saint Francis, that throngh his deserts, ne'er would I die an evil death. And so earnestly championed he my cause before the Lord Christ, that his prayers have obtained the grace of my soul's return to the body. Behold ! I have had a respite granted me, of twenty days, wherein to do penance for my sins; which days of grace being past, I shall surely die once more. And thus it befell within the period aforesaid, that the Bishop repurchased the goods which his kinsmen had taken away, and he devised the remainder of his possessions in virtuous and worthy fashion, and did condign penance for his faults. And whereas the festival of the Exaltation of the blessed Francis fell within this time; upon that Day, behold he celebrated Mass, preaching before the assembled multitude, as hath been told. And with such fervour discoursed he of the spirit of Saint Francis in the homily aforesaid, that the Minor Brethren who until that time had been little known in those parts, were thereafter mightily esteemed and held in honour in the province.

And this Miracle was proclaimed by Brother Francesco da Giunpareta, in Santa Croce (34) upon Saint Francis's Day, anno M.CCC.XLIIIJ, and Brother Bartholomeo da Melano the Reader of Lucha, writ the same to Brother Lodovico the Reader of Florence; having learned it from one of our Minor Brethren who was present when the aforesaid Bishop rose again from the dead. To the praise of Christ.

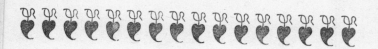

CHAPTER III.

HOW THE BLOOD FLOWED AFRESH FROM THE EFFIGY
OF SAINT FRANCIS (35).

EHOLD, in a certain Convent of the Friars Preachers, an effigy of Saint Francis with the Holy Stigmata was painted upon the Refectory wall. A certain Friar of the said Order, beguiled by the doubts begotten of pride in his heart, neither could nor would understand how it had come to pass that Saint Francis had received the most Holy Stigmata. Wherefore one day, when all the Brethren had withdrawn after their repast, this Friar strode up to the figure, hastily took away the Stigmata spoiling it, and went his way. Returning thither again upon the same day, Lo! he saw this effigy adorned with the Holy Stigmata more excellently than heretofore; whereupon, once more he defaced them with malice prepense, and, coming back again, he found the painting was repaired. Whereat, in his anger, this Friar damaged the figure once more, in such wise that the wall whereon it had been limned was bared entirely. And straightways from that wall, the blood gushed forth violently in exceeding abundance, even as the wine floweth from a full cask when the spigot is drawn; and splashed the face, the breast and the robe of the Friar, who fell terror-stricken to the ground, lifting up his voice and calling loudly for the Brethren. The entire community was aroused by his cries and hurried to the spot. Astounded and awestruck at the mighty prodigy they hastily collected the blood upon the ground most reverently with a sponge, and caused the said effigy to be repaired in most honourable fashion. And the elders commanded them that for the credit of the Rule, naught should they reveal thereof to any one outside their Order. Thereupon quoth that Friar: Rather will I be cast out from the Brotherhood, than conceal the wondrous marvel that honoureth Messer Saint Francis. Yet what requital did the lowlyminded Francis exact from this Friar? Naught else than that forthwith he made a new man of him; and in the fervour of his call he renounced all his books, and waxed great hereafter in prayer. And, awhile afterwards, drawing strength from the bosom of Saint Francis, he set forth upon a journey to his church of Ascesi (36), where in the presence of a number of the Friars Minor gathered together, humbling himself exceedingly and weeping many tears, he proclaimed the aforesaid Miracle shewing them, the blood that he had collected from the ground in the sponge.

A particle whereof he left with them in testimony of the prodigy, and he kept the remainder in blessed memory of Saint Francis. To the praise of Christ. Amen.

The healing of the Spanish nobleman. (Giotto di Bondone).

CHAPTER IV.

A MOST EXCELLENT MIRACLE OF THE STIGMATA
OF S. FRANCIS.

IN the kingdom of Castella (37) there dwelled a certain man, a devout votary of Saint Francis, who, hastening one day to the church of the Friars Minor to hear Compline was assailed by certain wicked men who fell upon him and without mercy whatsoever smote him cruelly, until he fell well-nigh lifeless at their feet. And these accurst ones departing thence, one of their number, most ruthless, thrust his knife into the man's neck in such wise that, unable to draw it forth afterwards, they went their way all together abandoning him for a dead man. Whereat a mighty tumult rose amid the neighbours, and the cries drew many folk together; and by all was he mourned as one dead, for of hope of his life seemed there none. And they raised him up from the ground and bore him to his dwelling; and his kinsfolk were busied ordering all things needful for the burial. When behold! the hour of midnight approaching, the bell at the convent of the Friars Minor began to toll for Mattins. At the pealing thereof, his good-wife, minding her that he was wont to go and hear Mattins with the Minor Brethren, set up a mighty and mournful wailing crying aloud: Alack a day my lord, where is thy piety? whither hath thy fervour departed? Up with thee and to Mattins, in sooth the bell tolleth for thee! Aroused by her piteous accents he began to make certain motions with his hands, praying them to draw forth the knife that molested him and hindered his speech.

And of a sudden, the knife was sharply seized, by whom none could see and drawn from this man's throat, in the sight of all the bystanders; and he was straight ways made whole. And rising from his bed he opened his mouth in speech thus: Give ear unto me my kinsmen and well-beloved friends: behold the wondrous power of Saint Francis whose servant I have ever been, he hath left me but now. And behold he hath approached me with his most Holy Stigmata, and laying his wounded hands upon my sores the fragrance and balm of these hallowed Wounds have soothed and healed my hurt perfectly! Wherefore, howbeit I motioned to you to draw the knife from my throat because I was tongue-tied, Lo! Saint Francis, doing me no hurt, seized the knife drawing it forth; and, witness ye all, by rubbing the gash aforesaid with his hand, he hath made me whole. To the praise of Christ. Amen.

CHAPTER V.

A PRODIGY IN THE SIGHT OF ALL THE PEOPLE.

T came to pass, that Saint Francis sojourning in the city of Allessandria in Lombardy, he lodged with a worthy citizen who besought him to partake that evening, — as the Gospel teacheth — (38) of the food that should be set before him. And Saint Francis consenting thereto; this man, to render a greater courtesy to his guest, killed and dressed a capon, of those that be fatted and seven years old to boot. And they were seated at supper, when an unbeliever came to beg an alms for the love of God. Saint Francis, hearing the Hallowed Name of God spoken, took up a knife and carving a piece of this fowl sent it out to the beggar, for the love of God. This miscreant took the alms, yet ate not thereof, but secreted the gift with the intent to put Saint Francis to shame. Wherefore upon the next day, when Saint Francis was preaching to the multitude, this unbeliever drew forth the capon's leg, and exclaimed : Behold, my masters, the meat whereof this man, whom ye revere as a saint, doth eat, yea the alms which he gave me yester e'en. Whereupon the entire assemblage turned their faces to the speaker, and looking at the thing that he held in his grasp, with one voice they reproved him for a fool; inasmuch as it befell by Divine interposition, that no capon's leg but a luscious fish was seen by the people in that man's hands. Lo! the miscreant stood abashed and repentant at the sight of so mighty a prodigy. And whereas in the presence of the multitude confessed he the error of his ways and was converted; behold! the meat was restored to its nature, even as he that bore false witness returned to his better self. To the praise of Christ. Amen.

CHAPTER VI.

HOW SAINT FRANCIS FIRST SENT THE BRETHREN INTO ENG-
LAND, AND THE MIGHTY WONDER THAT CHRIST VOUCH-
SAFED TO THEM UPON THE WAY THITHER.

BROTHER Angnolo of Pisa had been vested by
Saint Francis, and appointed Minister to England; and with him went Brother Alberto of
Pisa and three other Friars their companions (39). Coming to the city of Canturia (40) upon the third day
of May, they were most charitably entertained by the
Friars Preachers. And speeding onwards, they entered
a mighty darksome forest wherein the Black Monks
had a monastery. And howbeit the hour of Vespers was
at hand, and the weather with rain most inclement, their
garments being drenched and their strength sore spent;
these Friars craved shelter for the love of God lest
they perish through cold or through hunger, or by as-
sault of the wild beasts in that forest. The Porter, look
ing at those Friars whose haggard mien bespoke their
chastening, their shapeless and uncouth garb, and understanding not their tongue, imagined them to be
mummers and strolling players; and in this wise described he them to the Prior who had come at that season

with four Monks to take his ease at the grange. Upon
their being carried within, into the presence of the Prior
and his Monks, the Friars protested that no mummers or
strolling players were they, but rather the Lord's servants,
heralds of the Kingdom of Heaven, and fellows of the
Order of Apostles. And the Prior and the Monks commanded that even as rogues, beggars and vagabonds they be
driven forth from the Monastery gate, and that no bread
should they have, nor wine, nor shelter; or any mercy
whatsoever. And the younger of those Monks, marking
such hardheartedness, was moved to pity; and he went
after them, and besought the Porter, for brotherly kind-
ness' sake, to admit them privily and shelter them in
the hayloft; whither he would bring them food. Whereat
the Porter, hearkening to this young Monk's prayers,
put the Friars inside this loft or rather barn; and the
Monk came to them by stealth, and brought wine (41)
and bread and other things needful; thereafter visiting
them and commending himself most devoutly to their
prayers.

Behold in the night, the Monk aforesaid had this vision vouchsafed to him: Lo! he saw a wondrous shining
throne within a church, whereon sat the Blessed Lord
Christ, and many folk were being called up to judgment
before Him. And Christ bent a most terrible brow upon
them and spake thus: Let the masters of that grange
come before Me. Whereupon, forthwith the said Prior and
those IIII. Monks were so led thither. And there stepped
forward facing them a little poor man, meek and of lowly
countenance, wearing upon his shoulders the habit of
those sorry little Friars of whom hath been told, and
he lifted up his voice saying: O Judge most upright,

the wailing and the voice of the Minor Brethren's blood
that hath been spilled in this night, and to whom bodily
sustenance and shelter were denied in this Monastery,
cry vengeance unto Thee; howbeit for the love of Thee,
forsook they the world, and all bodily solace. And hither
have they come, seeking to recall these erring souls to
Thee my Lord, Who hast redeemed them with Thy precious Blood upon the Rood of the ✠; and this man
here present hath bidden them be driven forth without
the gate, even as mummers and strolling players. Whereupon Christ turned towards the Prior, with angered
mien and spake thus: Of whose Order beest thou, Prior?
He answered: Of the Order of Saint Benedict. And
Christ queried of Saint Benedict: Is that which this man
sayeth, true? Saint Benedict made answer: Verily, my
sweet Lord, this man with his companions is a destroyer
and wrecker of mine Order, even as hath been shewn in
the entertainment of those Minor Brethren Thy perfect
servants; inasmuch as I command in my Rule, that never
should the Abbot's table lack the presence of pilgrims
and needy wayfarers. And the manner of this man's obedience, Thou, My Lord, seest. Whereupon Christ delivered
judgment upon them: that they be hanged by the neck
from an elm-tree that grew there in the cloister. And they
being thus hanged, the Prior and three of his companions;
Christ turned to the fourth, he that had shewn mercy,
and spake thus: And thou, which be thine Order? The
youth quaking with fear, having listened how Saint Benedict had cast them from him, replied in fear and trem-
bling: My Lord, of this little poor man's Order am I.
Thereupon Christ called upon him by his name, and
said: Francis, doth this man belong to thine Order? And

Saint Francis answered: My Lord, he is of mine indeed, and thus from this hour do I hold him for my Brother. And he took and folded him in his arms most tenderly. And in that embrace the monk awoke in amazement at the vision, and most exceedingly also, that in his sleep he had heard the name of Francis first uttered by Christ's very self.

And marvelling thereat, lo! he rises hastily to make known to the Prior the matters thus vouchsafed to him in this vision. And he goeth to his chamber, and entering within, lo! he beholdeth this wicked little Prior strangled, and his body maimed, disfigured, and corrupt.

He runneth thence to his brethren, and similarly findeth he them throttled, and their bodies all undone. And he hasteneth speedily to the Friars to announce the prodigy; and behold the Porter, fearing the Prior's anger, had driven them forth before day-break.

Whereupon this Monk made all speed to relate these marvels to the Abbot of Abindon (42) and the Abbot hearkening to the young Monk's tale, felt an exceeding fear thereat, and together with his companions wondered they greatly.

Behold the tidings thereof spread well-nigh throughout the country, and those blessed Friars came to the City of Assonia (43); where, appearing before King Henry (44), they were welcomed by him most graciously, and he made them a free grant of land for their Monastery. And it came to pass that the holiness of those Friars and the unheard of prodigy wrought upon their behalf enhanced their fame throughout England; wherefore not alone this Monk whom Saint Francis had saved from so dire a penalty, became a Friar, and he

Saint Francis and his Twelve Companions. (Tiberio d'Assisi).

was the first, (45) but many others besides. Amongst
whom were a mighty Bishop, and an Abbot who out of
piety and exceeding lowliness bore the stones and the
water-barrel upon their back, — yea the Bishop and the
Abbot — for the building of the Monastery.

This Brother Agnolo, when he come to England, was
a youth of amiable parts and great piety aged XXX.
years; and being a deacon he would not be consecrated
or advanced to priest's orders, without leave from the
Chapter General. And thereafter, when the Archbishop
of Conturbia (46), through his Archdeacon, summoned
those that were to be ordained, he would exclaim: " Let
them come hither the Brethren of the Order of Apostles ".
And this name endured for many a long day in England.
Behold this Brother Agnolo travelled far and wide in
the Province preaching with exceeding fervour, and he
founded and built diverse monasteries and communities
of the Brethren, receiving many into the Order. Whereafter having compassed manifold wonders in his lifetime and after death also, he gave up his soul to his
Maker upon the day following the festival of Saint Gregory the Pope (47), and he is buried at Assonia (48). To
the praise of Our Lord Christ. Amen.

CHAPTER VII.

OF THE ADMIRABLE CONVERSION OF A CERTAIN WICKEDLY STIFF-NECKED MAN OF SPOLETO.

IN the city of Spoleto there lived a certain wicked and hard-hearted man whom no persuasion or argument in the world could reconcile with or cause to endure the sight of the Minor Friars; and least of all when they would come to him for alms. This man did curse and revile them, rejoicing in heaping insult upon them, and he would pursue them with mocking words and many jeers of lewdness and ribaldry. Wherefore the Brethren carried their grievance to Saint Francis who at that time had taken up his abode in the aforesaid monastery of Spoleto. And Saint Francis called Brother Andrea da Siena to him; he that was accustomed to go almost daily in quest of a dole, and spoke thus: " Go thou and seek by all means how thou mayest obtain an alms from this most hard-hearted of men. Brother Andrea, true to the dictate of holy obedience, goeth thither and so earnestly importuneth the churl; that not for compassion's sake but to rid himself of the beggar, did he give Brother Andrea an alms of bread, flouting him rudely and casting it at him from afar as is done to a dog. Brother Andrea took the gift, and returned rejoicing and glad of heart to Saint Francis and proffered the bounty aforesaid. And Saint Francis took the alms of bread and shared it amongst the Brethren giving a small piece thereof to each and said : " Go ye now, let each one of you repeat the Lord's Prayer three times, and beseech Him to convert and turn the steps of this sinner to the path of truth. Behold a marvel ! ere yet the Brethren had risen from supper, lo ! the churl cometh trudging to the Monastery, devoutly and with contrite heart ; and casteth himself at the feet of Saint Francis weeping many tears, confessing the error of his blindness before all the Brethren. And thereafter, putting on the new man he grew a kindly spirit, and became the friend and signal benefactor of the Minor Fiars. To the praise of Our Lord Christ. Amen.

CHAPTER VIII.

A PRODIGY OF EXCEEDING WONDERMENT, HOW CHRIST, IN
THE ARMS OF HIS SWEET MOTHER, BLESSED THE MUL-
TITUDE GATHERED TOGETHER IN THE DAYS OF THE
INDULGENCE IN SANTA MARIA DEGLI ANGELI.

N the days of the Indulgence, Anno Domini,
M.CCC.IIJ, the people having assembled in
the Church of Santa Maria degli Angeli as
in customary in this night of the Pardon; of a sudden
there arose a great clamour amongst them, even as hap-
peneth when some mighty portent occurs. Whereat the
Brethren, who were taking their rest upon the porch over
the door, together with the sleeping multitude, awoke;
and running hither and thither to learn what the uproar
might portend, naught saw they save a dove, passing
white, fly swiftly V. times round the church. And the
tumult and uproar prevailing, a certain Friar, Francisco Coçço, being minded to learn the true inwardness
of this thing, came down from the porch, and hied him
to Brother Currado of holy memory, — and his wonder-
working remains be interred in the Island Monastery (49)
—, whom he found in prayer before the altar: And he
spoke to him thus: " Well-beloved Father, even as
thou hearest, a great tumult and clamour hath arisen

amongst this multitude as though some prodigy hath appeared in their sight. Brother Currado replied: " My son, I charge thee so long as I live, that thou makest not known to any-one the things I am about to vouchsafe to thee. Lo! I have seen the Blessed Virgin Mary wrapt in plendour and a radiancy most wonderful, descend from Heaven's sublime height; she was holding her sweetest and most hallowed son, Christ, in her arms. And He blessed the multitude that come hither devoutly to gain this holy Indulgence: Wherefore the sweet Lord Christ having with His own hands given them His grace and benison, behold, the people were moved mightily and lifted up their voice in loud wonderment. To the praise of Our Lord Christ. Amen.

CHAPTER IX.

ANOTHER MIGHTY PRODIGY OF THE BLESSED INDULGENCE.

 certain nobleman of Apulia, whose name was
Francesco, preparing, Anno Dom., M.CCC.VIIJ,
to journey with his train to Santa Maria degli
Angeli for the Indulgence, said to one of his hinds who
had served him for a wage well-nigh throughout the
year: " How now my friend, why dost not thou labour
for thy soul's health, even as thou workest for thy bodily weal? " And he answered: " And how shall I labour
for my soul? " Quoth the nobleman: So thou comest
together with us to Saint Francis, there shalt thou find
remission of all thy sins. And the varlet made answer:
" Right willingly will I go thither together with you,
if you will pay me my wage for all the days that I
have toiled for you. Whereupon Messer Francesco paid
him in full; and setting forth all together with the hind
and the rest of his company they journeyed devoutly to
Saint Francis (shrine), where shriven and contrite, with
exceeding gladness of the spirit, they partook of the Indulgence in Santa Maria degli Angeli. And no sooner
had they set forth from Ascesi, upon their homeward
journey to Apulia, than the servant aforesaid sickened,
and thus sorely that his feet swelled and he could not

move a foot. Whereupon murmuring at the journey he had gone, the hind accosted Messer Francesco saying : " Would to God, that I had never come hither for this Indulgence, here have I spent those few monies that I had, and I am fallen sick; and all of you return to your homes, whilst I sorry wretch, remain behind alone, poverty and palsy-stricken. Messer Francesco answered : " I pray thee repent not of the singular favours which thou hast gained ". Yet the churl persisting that rather had he not come thither; quoth Messer Francesco: " Give me then the Indulgence, even so as thou receivedst it upon thine entrance into the church of Santa Maria degli Angeli, for my brother who is dead ; and I promise to repay thee all thou hast expended upon this quest, in the presence of these our comrades. And moreover, I will carry thee on my horse upon a pillion behind me, at mine own cost until we reach our home. A gainer as he thought thereby, the varlet endorses the bargain and receives the monies ; and, mounting the (nobleman's) horse rejoicing mightily, rideth upon his way. And Messer Francesco journeying thus together with the varlet and the others of his train, Lo ! the Knight's brother, that had died several months before appeared at noontide in their midst, and accosted them saying : " Oh sweetest brother mine, verily I thank thee for the signal favour which I have received at thy hands today, inasmuch as the blessed Indulgence that thou hast, of thy charity, purchased for me, hath delivered my soul from all the pains of Purgatory ; and, so thou shalt believe these my words are true, I will tell thee the happenings in thy household, from the day of thy departure thence. Learn therefore that thy house without the walls hath been broken into by robbers, and one of thy bullocks hath been maimed of a foot, and thy servants are in sore perplexity. They await thy coming. And thy household and thy kinsfolk and thy frieeds, shall travel several miles to meet thee. Withal to grieve thee not, naught thereof will they reveal to thee : But, tarry thou not to learn their tidings forthwith, an so thou findest my words are true, mayest thou of a surety believe that the blessed Indulgence of Porziuncula hath delivered me from all pain, and I dwell in Paradise this day. And so speaking was he seen no more.

This Knight having seen and heard all these things, pondereth diligently thereon ; and maketh speed joyfully towards his home ; when, approaching his demesne some three miles, behold his kinsfolk and friends coming forward with every mark of welcome and rejoicing. The Knight with seeming eagerness queries : " How fare they all at home ? Be there any new happenings therein since I departed me to Ascesi ? " And those kinsfolk answered : " We shall tell thee all when thou crossest thy threshold and thou wilt see for thyself. Quoth Messer Francesco ; " Forsooth not one step farther will I go an I learn not all things. Lo ! I speak not unadvisedly. Whereupon his kinsmen unfolded their tidings in order, even as his brother had revealed to him, when he had appeared by the road-side before their eyes. Whereat Messer Francesco lifted up a joyful countenance and exclaimed : " Now indeed do I know and firmly believe, that the Indulgence of Santa Maria degli Angeli whereby my beloved brother hath entered into the joys of paradise, is most real and pleasing in the sight of God Almighty. To the praise of Our Lord Christ. Amen.

The Sermon of the Birds – Monte Subasio. (Benozzo Gozzoli).

CHAPTER X.

HOW SAINT DOMINIC BORE TESTIMONY
TO THE INDULGENCE OF SANTA MARIA DEGLI ANGELI.

 certain woman from La Magna (50), come to
the Pardon of Santa Maria da Porziuncula,
testified and made oath, to witness a number
of the Brethren and many secular clergy, before the altar
of Saint Francis; and Merlino interpreted her words —
which the said Merlino was of Ascesi, — that she had in
very sooth beheld this prodigy of the hallowed Indulgence. Thus speaking quoth she: " I Ysa, being minded
many a long year since to come hither for the blessed
Indulgence, and manifold hindrances besetting me, have I
delayed my coming until this very day. At last having
ordered and made ready all things needful for my journey,
I betook myself to the church of the Friars Preachers
hard by my home; and summoning my confessor I asked
for the sacrament of Penance, laying firstly before him
how I was minded to journey to Saint Francis'(shrine)
for the Indulgence which is to be gained in Santa Maria
degli Angeli. Whereat this Friar, angered and indignant,
would not shrive me nor grant me leave to come hither
saying, that there was no such Indulgence as had been

7

said. Wherefore, much distressed, I turned my steps homewards sorrowing bitterly; and thus grieving, I encountered two Friars Preachers who spoke to me: " Why art thou thus saddened? " And I answered them, shewing cause. Quoth they: " Be of good cheer and grieve no more, but turn back with us to the Monastery, and for thy soul's comfort will we find thee a good confessor". And I went thither with them and they made good their word; and I was shriven. Behold! those two Friars summoned a number of the Brethren in the convent; to whom being assembled in my presence, one of those two spake thus: " Well-beloved Brethren all, hold ye for certain without hesitancy whatsoever, that the Indulgence of Santa Maria degli Angeli is real and true, and holier far in the sight of God Almighty than is commonly believed; and, that ye may credit my words, know ye that I am Saint Dominic your Father and the first founder of this Order, and this (my companion) is Saint Peter Martyr ". And having spoken those words they forthwith vanished from our sight. Wherefore, so mighty a prodigy having been vouchsafed to me, I straightways set out upon my journey, and have come hither, even as ye behold me, to gain this most blessed and holy Indulgence. To the praise of Our Blessed Lord Christ Jesu. Amen.

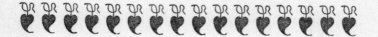

CHAPTER XI.

THAT Emperor of Constantinople whose name was John, became a Minor Friar after this wise. The sands of his life had well-nigh run out, and having enjoyed singular happines and worldly prosperity therein, and marking how old age was steal-ing upon him; behold him meditating upon death. And, t'is thought, the Lord put a craving into his heart to know what manner of an end he should make. And the desire waxing hot within him, lo! in his sleep he had this vision vouchsafed to him. He beheld a certain ve-nerable sage clothed in white robes, standing before him, holding the habit of the Friars Minor with their sandals and cord in his hand; who calling him by his name: "Emperor John quoth he, so thy heart desireth "thus eagerly to learn the manner of thine ending, know "thou that under this garb of the Friars Minor wilt thou "close thine eyes, for in sooth such is the Divine Will". The Emperor awakening, marvelled at the indignity which should compel him to quit the empire's sway, to humble

himself as a Minor Brother. By no means upon earth
would his soul assent thereto. Wherefore, as though in
self-pity being well-nigh moved to tears, he uttered
loud sighs; and his wailing accents drew the chamberlains
and courtiers to his side, who queried the cause of his
sorrowful grieving, yet naught thereof would he reveal. In
the night thereafter, two men, likewise garbed in white
robes, appeared before the Emperor in his sleep, with
the habit and the cord and the sandals, saying: " Thus
" saith the Lord, die thou shalt under this robe ". Whereat
as heretofore a mighty fear overcame him, and the plaint
of his woeful cries called the courtiers once more to his
side, yet again would he not tell them the cause of his
distress. Behold in the third night, three men robed in
white garments and of mien most venerable, holding
the habit, the sandals and the cord, stood before the Emperor in his sleep; saying and repeating how he should
die in very sooth under that robe, such being the Lord's
Will; and they added; " Nay, deem not this sign a fond
" fancy or vain dream; for even as we say unto thee so
" shall it surely come to pass, without let or hindrance ".
The Emperor awakening, he commanded that his confessor Brother Angelo be summoned; who, hastening
to his side, found the Emperor in the presence-chambe
weeping bitterly. Quoth Brother Angelo thereupon: " Ve-
" rily am I acquainted with the cause of thy sorrow, for
" the vision which the Lord vouchsafed to thee, hath
" been revealed to me likewise, and thou mayest assuredly
" reckon that He hath determined how thou shalt end thy
" days, and die under the garb of the Friars Minor ". And
(he comforted) the Emperor, laying to his heart diverse
ensamples of exceeding lowliness, and how humility is a

virtue most pleasing to the Lord; forasmuch as a man humbleth himself in this world, so shall He exalt him in Paradise. Whereafter a space of days having elapsed, he sickened of an tertian ague, and in obedience to the Divine purpose, that had thrice been shewn to him in a dream; behold this Emperor, deliberately, and with every mark of piety and lowliness, and despite the many tears of the bystanders; entered the Order of Saint Francis, and therein ended he his days most worthily.

And whereas sometimes the Brethren would gainsay him the performance of the humbler offices, to wit, his going forth to seek alms, the cleansing of their platters, or the sweeping out of their dwelling; he would repeat this prayer which he hath writ, most devoutly: " O sweet " my Lord Christ Jesus, grant me grace that having lived " my days in the world's pomps, clad in vain and precious " raiment, I may please Thee by going with the wallet " round my neck begging for alms, and follow Thee who " for my sake didst humble Thyself in poverty in this " world, to give me life eternal ".

The prayer aforesaid was heard favourably by the Lord, forasmuch as this Emperor set the Brethren an example of exceeding lowliness, and he passed out of this life full of virtues and the grace of God, into Paradise.

A llaude Christi. Amen.

S. Bonaventura. (Benozzo Gozzoli).

NOTES.

(1) Cf. L. MANZONI, ' Di una nuova edizione dei Fioretti di S. Francesco....' etc. Reg. Tip. Bologna, 1887. The Mss. (c. pp. 81-120) are preserved :

1-2. Rome, Vatican Lib. Coll. Capponiana, N. 184, and Corsini Lib. Cod. 44. F. 36.

3. Naples, Coll. Cav. Bruno Fabricatore.

4-5. Florence, Riccardian Lib. Nos., 1670-1781

6-7. Padua, Bib. del Seminario, Cod. N. 34. Bib. del Santo, Scaff. XI, 22.

8. Venice, Bib. di S. Marco, N. 40. Cod. cl. I, N. IX.

The discrepancies in the text, and the variants in the number and sequence of the additional Ensamples in the several Mss. are noted and described by Manzoni (op. cit. p. 81-120). Cf. LUIGI MANZONI, ' Studi sui Fioretti di S. Francesco ', pub. in the Miscellanea Francescana. Vols. III-IV. Foligno, 1888-9.

(2) ' Il Propugnatore ', N. S., vol. I, p. Iª, pp. 396-411. ' Nove capitoli inediti dei Fioretti di S. Francesco ' pubblicati da GUIDO MAZZONI. The Ms. (Biblioteca del Santo, Scaff. XI, 22), is finely engrossed in XVth Century cursive script, in octavo. The text of the Fioretti is identical with that of the printed versions, and the sequence of the Chapters follows the same order, under the heading : " Al " nome di Cristo crucifixo e de la sua madre gloriosa vergine Maria. " In questo libro si contiengono certi miracholi et exempli devoti del " glorioso poveretto de Cristo, Misier San francescho e de alquanti soi " frati e compagni devotissime ". The additional Ensamples are entitled ? " Istoria del santo nome de la Vernia e de le sante stimate del beatissimo padre santo francescho ". The dedicatory " envoi " fur-

nishes us with the name and birthplace of the copyist, one Johan franciscus de lusia, notarius et civis Feltrensis. " Deo dante explevit " hoc opus ad istanciam domine Elisabeth uxoris q. viri nobilis q. Ro- " magni de Romagno Civis Feltrensis Curenti Anno Domini MCCCCLJ. " Indictione xiiij die vero primo mensis aprilis. Finis. Laus Deo crea- " tori nostro et gloriose Virgini matris marie Sanctissimoque Fran- " cischo ".

(3) MANZONI (op. cit., p. 56-73) was acquainted with but three MSS. of the Antiqua Legenda:

I. Vatican Lib., N. 4354. The MS. a small 4º vol., with parchment covers, the latin text in cursive XIVth century script. Abbreviations render decyphering difficult. The title written in red, runs: " incipit Antiqua Legenda.... etc. The volume consists of 157 paper leaves measuring about 22 ½ × 15 centimetres. This MS. which seems to have escaped the notice of most earlier historians of S. Francis, is mentioned in a note in Carlo Fea's: ' Descrizione ragionata della sacrosancta patriarcal basilica e Capella papale di S. Francesco d'Assisi '. Roma, 1820; Tip. Camerale.

II. A XVth Cent. MS., in the Lib. of the Convent of S. Isidoro, at Rome, dated at the end of the volume, 1443 die 2 septembris. The MS. marked 1/82, is a small 8º paper volume, bound in parchment. The text which diverges notably from that of the Vatican (Latin) MS. is written in cursive script of marked German type, " and " indeed says count Manzoni, there can be small doubt of the copyists " nationality ".

III. The MS. in the Vatican Library, Ottoboni Collection, N. 681. This XVth Century MS., a small 8º volume of 306 pages, consists of miscellaneous writings commencing with the Sayings of Br. Egidio, (p. 1-33); and a Treatise by S. Bonaventure, ending (p. 54) with the Chapter on Holy Poverty. On p. 55. we have an Italian translation by a Venetian scribe of the Antiqua Legenda, written in indifferent script: Comenza la vita di S. Francesco; ending on p. 106, with the chapter numbered 63 in the Latin version. Here the writer of the first part of the MS. reappears, transcribing in a single Chapter various episodes of the life of S. Francis, and several Homilies by S. Bonaventure, a Treatise by Fr. Jacopo da Todi, and a number of Laude.

(4) Cf. L. MANZONI, ' Di una nuova edizione dei Fioretti di San Francesco, secondo il testo di Amaretto Manelli '. Bologna, Re-

gia Tip., 1887. " This XIV th century MS. of the Fioretti, (Racc.
Pal. Cod. E. 5. 9. '84, was discovered by Ct. Manzoni in the National
Library at Florence some forty one years since. He is inclined to
see in Amaretto Manelli the first translator, as well as the first known
copyist of the Fioretti. The text is beautifully engrossed in very le-
gible cursive script without mistakes or erasures, upon 120 small quarto
paper leaves. Twenty-nine to thirty lines cover the pages, measuring
15 $\frac{1}{2}$ × 9 $\frac{1}{2}$ centimètres, with inside and outside margins of equal
width. The text opens as follows : " Al nome di Cristo a dì 31 di
" Maggio 1396, la vigilia della Pasqua dello chorpo suo cominciano
" i fioretti di Sancto francescho "; and ends with the words : " Iscritto
" e ichonpiuto per me amaretto, Lunedì a dì xvij de Luglio anno
" domini MCCCLXXXXVI sonando vespro poco dopo le xviiij ore,
" a Dio sia onore et grolia Amen ". Amaretto di Zenobi Manelli who
tells us naively " how he commenced his task upon the vigil of Corpus-
christi, finishing ths work, at the stroke of vespers, a little after
the 19th hour, on July 15 th ", was a well-to-do citizen of Florence.
He joined the ranks of the Popolari on October 9 th 1361, and was
knighted in 1380. The family adopted the surname of de' Pontigiani
from their houses situated by the Ponte Vecchio in the Oltr'Arno
quarter. A scholar and copyist of rare merit and accuracy, Amaretto
Manelli was also the author of an historical work called " Crona-
chette Antiche ", which but for the disappearance of the original MS.,
would have set at rest genealogical doubts and questions raised by the
erroneous assertions of his 18 th Century biographer and editor Do-
menico Maria Manni.

(5) ' I Fioretti del Glorioso Messere Santo Francesco e de' suoi
Frati '. A cura di G. L. PASSERINI. Firenze, Sansoni. 1903. The MS.
preserved in the Riccardian Library at Florence (N. 1670) is written
in bandsome XV th century Gothic script (black-letter), in double co-
lumn, with illuminated initial letters and chapter-headings in colour.
The 190 leaves measure 290 × 215 millim., and contain besides the
Fioretti Chapters also the Life of S. Francis, the Rule of the Friars,
the Last Testament of the blessed Messere S. Francis, and two fine
Laude. The additional Ensamples : under the heading " Here are set
forth certain fine ensamples and miracles of Messer S. Francis ", are
bound up at the end of the volume, but their position according to
the index should have been between the Franciscan Rule and the
Fioretti Chapters.

8

(6) Neither of the two recent and authoritative English translations of the Fioretti ; viz : Mr. Heywood's admirable version of the " Little Flowers " (Methuen) and that of Prof. Arnold, (Chatto & Windus) contain this additional matter.

(7) Cf. ' Arch. Fran. Hist.'. Ann. I, fasc. I, Bibliographia (p. 133), P. MICHEL BIHL, O. F. M. " Après les scripta B. Francisci " viennent les biographies proprement dites. M. Joergensen en distingue quatre groupes. Il parle d'un groupe Celano (c. 1230), Leone (1245 c.), S, Bonaventure (c. 1265), et enfin d'un groupe Speculum (c. 1320ss.). Le premier est formé par la Vita I. de Th. de Celano et de ses dépendances littéraires, en premier lieu la Legende de Fr. Julien de Spire... La deuxième classe embrasse la Legenda Trium Sociorum, le soi disant Anonymus Perusinus et la Vita II. de Celano.... le troisième groupe comprend les Légendes de S. Bonaventure et le Liber de Laudibus de Fr. Bernard de Besse.... La dernière classe se compose du Speculum perfectionis, (écrit selon M. Joergensen non en 1227, mais en 1318) de la Legenda Antiqua et des Actus Fioretti. Cf. also (pp. 84-106) the recent and authoritative work by Prof. J. Joergensen. Der heilage Franz von Assisi : (Pub. Jos. Kösel, Kempten and Munich, 1908), translated from the danish by Ctesse H. Holstein Ledrebor̄g referred to by P. Michel Bihl.

(8) Supplementum et castigatio ad scriptores Minorum Ordinum a Waddingho aliisque descriptos. Romae 1806, apud Linum contendi. Fr. Jo. Hyacinthus Sbaralea is quoted by Manzoni in reference to Frate Fabiano Ungaro, the compiler of the Speculum Vitae Beati Francisci ; concerning whose writings see also Joergensen (op. cit., pp. 130 et seq.). The compiler tells us his name ; when speaking of himself " he prays the Lord to bless and keep him Frate Fabiano, taking pity upon him to turn His countenance upon him ". (Quoted from Manzoni's reference to the edition printed, Venice, 1504).

(9) MANZONI, ' Studi sui Fioretti....', (op. cit.) quotes also the Annales Minorum compiled by Wadding. Vol. VI, Romae typis Rochi Bernabo, 1703. " Erat hoc tempore 1319, Archiepiscopus Ecclesia Rigiensis in Livoniae Metropolitana frater Fredricus Minorita, uti constat ex literis pontificiis. Quia presentis.... datis ". Sbaralea mentions the archbishop under the heading Fredricus Teutonicus and give the date of his death in the year 1330. Joergensen callis him " Friedrich Barov " and gives the date of his death as occurring in 1340. Another passage of the Speculum relates how the writer Frate Fa-

biano began his work at Avignon where as a youth he studied under the Archbishop. " In imis cum essem studens in Avignone recepi quorum aliquid pro mea devotione et exercitia monendo sed potius excucienda pigritia collegi et.... annotavi. " Now if Archbishop Frederic who governed the See of Reims 1316-18, sojourned with the Brethren before procceding tho is new and distant diocese, there seems nohing improbable in Manzoni's view that the compiler of the Speculum and the Antiqua Legenda is that same, novice who sate at the Bishop's feet taking down the " history of those whose acts are hallowed and their names be writ in the Book of Life ".

(10) ' The Chronicle of Thomas of Eccleston '. " De adventu Fratrum Minorum in Angliam.... with preface and notes by Father Cuthbert, O. S. F. C. Sands e Co. London, 1909.

(11) Cf. Some chronological difficulties in the Life of S. Francis of Assisi. P. PASCHAL ROBINSON, O. F. M. in ' Arch. Fran. Hist. '. " Item, praecepit Generale Capitulum ' per obedientiam ', quod omnes legendae de beato Francisco olim factae deleantur et ubi inveniri poterunt extra Ordinem, ipsas Fratres studeant amovere, cum illa legenda, quae facta est per Generalem, sit compilata, prout ipse habuit ab ore illorum, qui cum Beato Francisco quasi semper fuerunt, et cuncta certitudinaliter scriverint, et omnia ibi sint posita diligenter ".

(12) Cf. F. P. ROBINSON, Op. cit. " For several centuries this same Legend (The Legenda Maior of S. Bonaventure) was the only XIIIth century biography of S. Francis in circulation.... it held the field, and subsequent Lives of the Saint were drawn mainly from this source, with such occasional references to such scraps of the Ancient Legend, (i. e. that of the Three Companions) as had in one way or another been preserved ".

(13) S. Bonaventure tells us, writes P. ROBINSON (op. cit.) that : " in " order to avoid confusion he has not always woven together the hi- " story of S. Francis according to the order of time, but has studied " rather to follow a more coherent order ; setting down facts of divers " kinds that belong to the same period, or facts of the same kind that " belong to divers periods, according as they seemed to fit in together. ' Such then was S. Bonaventure's method.... a typical example of me- ' dieval chronology.... It must be evident, therefore, that his Legend, " notwithstanding its immense value and importance in other respects, " can hardly serve as a solid basis for a scientific chronology of the " life of S. Francis. We must remenber that the early biographers

" wrote according to the temper of their time, and the point of view
" of the thirteenth century was not that of the twentieth in so far
" at least as hagiography is concerned...? ". They were satisfied to
" act upon the edict of the Chapter which prescribed the course they
" were to follow. " They did not care if the exact dates in a Saints life
" were not under the eyes of their readers provided a vivifying spirit
" entered theis readers souls.... their primary aim was to edifiy. This
" is why they are so comparatively oblivious to everything save what
" actually tends to establish and exalt the sanctity of those of whom
" they write and why the historical features which.... we have come
" to regard as essential to a complete grasp of the subject seem to
" have had little interest for them,... Biographers did not as a rule,
" adhere to the chronological order of the events they recorded, or
" attempt to determine the interval between them ; often they inverted
" the order to suit their purpose.... This practise of theirs may also
" furnish an important clue towards clearing up not a few of the
" seeming inconsistencies or contradictions in the order of events found
" in the early writings ". For instance " a glance through S. Bona-
" venture's Legenda Maior shews how he followed the order he con-
" siders more congruous. After treating of the institution of the Third
" Order (which tradition ascribes to 1221), he relates the foundation
" of the Clares (which is usually referred to 1212), he next passes on
" to speak of the cure of Fra Morico (1209 ?), the vocation of Fra
" Pacifico (1212-1213 ?), of the Chapter of Mats (1217-19-20-21) and
" that of Arles (1224), of the approbation of the Rule by Honorius III
" (29 th Nov. 1223); and then adds " a very few days afterward " the
" Stigmata were impressd upon the body of S. Francis (c. Sept. 4 th
" 1224). As a matter of fact nearly ten months intervened between
" the two last events. And all these facts are recerded without even
" an approximate date ".

(14) The Speculum Perfectionis was edited for the first time in
modern days by Prof. SABATIER, and published by him in the original
Latin in 1898 (Paris, Fischbacher). An English traslation by M.r Se-
bastian Evans appeared in tke following year, (David Nutt, London).
The attribution of the Speculum writings in their present form to
Brother Leone, has I believe now been generally abandoned by authoritative opinion upon the Primitive Franciscan Legendary writings.

(15) Cf. ' Arch. Fran. Hist., Ann. I, Fasc. I, Miscellanea ' (pp. 177-8)
P. ENRICO BULLETTI O. F. M. P. Bulletti reports the discovery of a

The Blessed John of Parma. (Benozzo Gozzoli).

Ms. copy of the Speculum Perfectionis in the Communal Library at Siena, which, were the early date assigned to the copy viz; — the first half of the XIV th century, to be accepted by paleographers, it should furnish students with a transcript almost contemporary with the original work.

The Siena Ms. described by P. Bulletti; is marked F. XI. 5. and consists, " of 48 leaves (numbered by another more modern hand); " measuring 232 X 164 mill., the pages are covered with easily decy- " pherable semigothic script. The Ms. is in a poor state of preser- " vation. The title headings and initial letters are executed in red " ink. The binding, a plain parchment cover, appears to have been " made out of a fragment of some Missal or Breviary, upon which " the following description has been traced : ' Questo Codice appar- " tenente già al soppresso Convento dell' Osservanza, passò nella Bi- " blioteca Comunale di Siena nell'anno 1869, essendo bibliotecario il " Dott. Francesco Grottanelli Cod. di C. 48 '. The Ms. is described " in the old Library Catalogues of the Convent of the Osservanza, " as well as in the supplementary Catalogue of the Siena Library ; " as a XIV th century Ms. text of the Admonitiones beati Francisci ; " containing under the heads :

I. - f. 1 r. - 4 r. Admonitiones B. Francisci.

II. - f. 4 r. - 5 r. Laudes quas ordinavit B. Franciscus et dicebat eas ad omnes horas.

III. - f. 5 r. - 8 v. Two epistles by S. Francis ; one addressed to the Chapter General, the other to the faithful. This is followed by the blessing accorded to Brother Leone.

IV. - f. 8 v. - 48. Speculum Perfectionis, commencing : " Incipit " Speculum Perfectionis fratris Minoris quod inferius continetur. — " Postquam quaedam regula quam fecerat B. Franciscus perdita fuit etc. " Explicit speculum perfectionis status fratris minoris in quo sunt (sic) " vocationes et perfection (sic) perfectionis posite (sic) sufficientissime " speculari. Omnis laus et gloria sit domino patri et filio et spiritui " sancto honor et gloria et gratiarum actio gloriosissime virgini " Marie. Amen.

A noteworty feature of this Ms., is the insertion between the last words of the Speculum text and the, ' explicit ', of a letter of. Saint Francis : " de modo servando circa fratres subditos peccantes morta- " liter venialiter ", beginning : " Fratri H. (Helias ?) ministro. ' Dominus " te benedicat, Dico tibi sicut possum, etc.... Et ista et omnia alia quae

9

" minus sunt in regula Domino Deo adiuvante procurabitis adimplere.
" Deo gratias. Amen '. A cursory comparison of this Ms., says P. Bul-
" letti, with the text published by Prof. Sabatier, and the Ognissanti
" copy (Ms.), reveals not a few discrepancies between these several
" documents ".

Cf. also the learned essay of P. B. Kruitwagen, O. F. M.: " De-
scriptio nonnullorum Codicum Mss. quibus insunt libelli Speculum Perfectionis..." etc. (pr. in Fasc. II-III of the Arch. Fran. Hist. p. 301-3),
who laments the disappearance of the XV th Century Antwerp and
Louvain Mss.

(16) Cf. La Leggenda di San Francesco scritta da tre suoi Compa-
gni, pubblicata per la prima volta nella sua vera integrità, dai PP. Mar-
cellino da Civezza e Teofilo Domenichelli dei Minori. Roma, Tip. ed.
Sallustiana MDCCCXCIX. The Three Companions, Frate Leone, Frate
Angelo and Frate Ruffino, were trusted friends and Disciples of the
Founder.

" The first twelve Brethren are : S. Francis, the Founder of the
" Order, who was joined two years later by Fr. Bernardo di Quinta-
" valle, the third was Fr. Pietro, the fourth Fr. Giulio, the fifth
" Fr. Sabbatino, the sixth Fr. Morice, the seventh Fr. Giovanni da
" Cappella, the eighth Fr. Filippo Longo, the first visitor of the Poor
" Ladies, the ninth Fr. Giovanni da San Constantio, the tenth Fr. Bar-
" bero, the eleventh Fr. Bernardo della Vite, the twelfth Fr. Agnolo
" di Tancredo ". (Cf. Chap. XII, Leg. 3, Soc.).

(17) Cf. The Lives of S. Francis of Assisi by Brother Thomas of
Celano Translated by A. G. Ferrers Howells. (Methuen) " Very little
" is known of the life of Thomas of Celano. He was a native of that
" town which lies on the southern border of the Abruzzi, in the dio-
" cese of Marsica and close to the now drained lake of Fucino.... He
" was probably admitted to the Order by S. Francis, some time between
" the years 1213-1216.... According to Fr. E. D'Alençon, he ended
" his days as spiritual director of a Monastery of Poor Clares near
" Tagliacozzo (about sixteen miles from Celano) where he was buried
" A prolific writer, several liturgical works are attributed to him, be-
" sides the two Lives of S. Francis and the Treatise upon Miracles ".

(18) Cf. ' Introduction, The Little Flowers of S. Francis. W. Heywood. ' (Methuen, London).

(19) Cf. F. CUTHBERT, (op. cit. pp. 1-6). " In the year of the Lord
1224, in the time of the Lord Pope Honorius.... the Friars Minor first

arrived in England..., They were four clerics and five lay Brethren....
On arriving at Canterbury they sojourned for two days at the Priory
of theHoly Trinity. Then four of them at once set of for London "·

The life story of the six foreign Brethren : Agnellus of Pisa, Henry
of Treviso, Lawrence of Beauvais, William of Florence, James ' from
beyond the Alps ', and Melioratus, is known; the identity of the hapless
brethren whose strange speech and uncouth appearance aroused the
suspicion of the Porter at the Priory gate, must therefore reamain a
mystery. John of Reading the Abbot of Osney (p. 25), was one of the
first to join the Friars, leaving his own Order for the purpose. For
the mention of Ralph Bishop of Hereford assisting in the building of
a house of the Friars, and carrying water and stones ". (Note 1, p. 2).

(20) Cf. ' The Book of Dignities (Allen & Co. London, 1894) p. 485;
also, p. 430. Stephen Langton Archbishop of Canterbury, 1207-1228.

(21) Cf. F. CUTHBERT, op. cit. pp. XXIII, Pref. also pp. 2, 8, 12,
21, 50, 60, 65, 66, 74, 98, 100; App. II (B), 139; App. III (B), 153.

(22) Cf. ' F. CUTHBERT op. cit. p. 140. App. II, Note 1. Albert
of Pisa was Minister in Germany at the time. The Chron. XXIV.
Gen. Glassberger (Anal. Franc. II, pp. 14-28), and Wadding (Annales
Minorum ad ann. 1223) all make the same mistake. Cf. also p. 100.
" But when Brother Elias heard from the messenger that Brother
Agnellus was dead.... he commanded (1236) Brother Albert of Pisa
to go to England to minister to the Brethren. Brother Albert had
been already Minister of Hungary, Germany, Bologna, and of the marches of Ancona, the marches of Treviso, and Tuscany. " Albert of Pisa
was elected Minister-General on May 15 th, 1239. He died about the
beginning of the following year ", circa festum Nativitatis Domini
" according to the Chron. Gen. XXIV., but on Jan. 23 rd according
to the Album Generale, wich also states that he died at Pisa and was
buried there ". (Note 1, op. cit. p. 86).

(23) Cf. F. CUTHBERT op. cit. Preface pp. XXIX-XXXII.

(24) Cf. GIOTTO. ' Künstler Monogr. Velhagen u. Klasing Bielefeld '
Leipzig, 1889. H. Thode. Despite Prof. Thode's enthusiastic apprecia-
tion (p. 21 et seq.) of the series of twenty eight frescoes in the nave
of the Upper Church at Assisi, depicting varions episodes in the Life
of S. Francis, critics are far from agreed in tracing the masters hand
in all the " histories ". The first of the series, and the group which
includes S. Francis's Sermon to the birds, the Death of the Lord of
Celano, S. Francis preaching before Honorius III, the Saint's appearance

at the Chapter at Arles, the Impression of the Stigmata, his Stigmata
the Death, the Vision of the Bishop of Assisi, the Verification of the
Salutation of the Procession with the Saint's bier, by S. Clare, and
the Canonization of S. Francis; exhibit, in P. B. Kleinschmid's; words
(cf. die Basilika S. Francesco in Assisi, in Arch. Fran. Hist. Ann. 1,
Fasc. II-III) " a marked superiority over the others; whilst the lean,
" and tall figures in the remaining four, display totally different types
" of portraiture ". The 27th " history ,,: the Spanish nobleman, who
is fallen upon by robbers, and left mortally wounded by the road-side is
only saved from death by the touch of the Saint's hand ; is depicted
with a masterly understanding of the by-standers feelings. The helpless
look of the Physician, and the reproving attitude of the Wife towards
her unconscious lord, tell their story as plainly as though the painting spoke.

(25) John of Brienne of Jerusalem. (1228-1237) co-regent and asso-
ciate Emperor with Baudwin II. a minor. " By the rude poets of the
" age, John of Brienne is compared to Hector, Roland and Judas
" Maccabaeus.... The Empire was soon deprived of the last of her
" champions; and the dying monarch was ambitious to enter Paradise
" in the habit of a Franciscan Friar ", (Decline and Fall of the Roman
Empire, Chap. LXI, Gibbon).

(26) Cf. Die Entstehung des Portiuncula Ablasses. P. H. Holzapfel
O. F. M. Arch. Fran. Hist. Ann. I. Quaracchi, 1908. In this most
scholarly essay the traditional view i. e. that the gift to S. Francis
can be historically asserted finds a supporter in the author. He ad-
duces cogent evidence in the testimony of Fr. Petrus Olivi the zea-
lous leader of the Spiritual Party. Born in or about the year 1248 in
the south of France, Olivi joined the Order at the age of twelve. He
is known to have studied in Paris and he sojourned in Rome during
several years in and after 1279. He was Reader in Florence in and
after 1287, and died at Montpellier on March 14th. eleven years later.
He left a Treatise embodying his views: " Quaestio hujusque inedita
de Indulgentia Portiunculae " which was only printed in 1895. This
work would appear to have been compiled either during his sojourn
in Rome or after the meeting with Fra Ubertino da Casale, another
early witness, who is known to have sojourned in Florence whither
he had come from Assisi, in 1287. The value of Olivi's testimony has
been variously estimated ; and if nothing else, it may be saide to establish conclusively the sanction extended to the " devotion " by eccle-

siastical authority from the earliest times. Pilgrimage to S. Maria degli Angeli had to Olivi's knowledge been a constant popular practise for many years before he committed his statement to writing. The general and annual frequentation of Assisi for the purpose of gaining the Indulgence can accordingly be carried back to 1250-60, Olivi does not recall a time when the Indulgence did not exist, and if his statement does not actually prove the personal grant to S. Francis it certainly sustains the traditional belief.

Another witness, Fr. Ubertino da Casale entered the Franciscan ranks in or about the year 1273 at the age of fourteen. At the age of twenty-eight or so he joirns the Community at Greccio ; coming afterwards to Rome where he meets their late General Br. Joanne of Parma who enjoins an early pilgrimage to Assisi upon his young disciple. He accordingly arrives there in time for the Indult, telling us: " Tunc romana sanctuaria visitans, et ad angelum faciei Iesu vere sanctissimum Ioannem de Parma ad Rupem deveniens laetus et ab ipso confortatus, absolutus et instructus in die indulgentiae, secundae diei Augusti intravi ecclesiam beatae Mariae de Portiuncula et iuxta eam pernoctavi ". He once more mentions his visit to Fr. Joanne : " in the fourth year before his death.... upon S. James's " Day, eight days before the first of August. " Fi. Joanne of Parma died on March 20 th, 1289, the Portiuncula visit may therefore be placed in 1285 ; and since Fra Ubertino did not come to Florence for two years the interval was probably spent " sub tituli studii, at Assisi. Fr. Ubertino's treatise : " Arbor vite crucifixe Jesu Christi, (1305, printed Venice 1485) contains besides copious biographical detail, references also to individuals sufficient to establish the accuracy of his recollections. The circumstance " that " S. Francis in person obtained from the Pope upon earth, the grant " of the Plenary Indulgence for his church, which the Blessed Virgin " Mary in Heaven, upon the second day of August had entreated of " her Divine Son, can only have been learned from Fr. Joanne ". Fra Ubertinos warranty, in the person of the latter strengthens the traditional position ; he had joined the Brotherhood as a youth so early as 1233, preceding S. Bonaventure in the Generalship, for the years 1247-1257. The " instruction " imparted by Fr. Joanne to his disciples doubtless followed tradition and in F. Holzapfel's view, the teacher being in a position to recall the earliest times, his testimony lends weight to the opinion generally shared that the Indulgence dates back to the Founder's life-time.

Thus whilst evidence abounds in respect of the popularity of the Festival in the latter years of the XIIIth century, the stamp of incontrovertible authenticity has not so far been set upon the Ms. signed statement by Fr. Benedict of Arezzo; which, were the date of the document uncontested, would set the question of the personal grant to S. Francis permanently at rest. Fr. Benedict of Arezzo was born late in the XIIth century. One of the first to enter the Order, he was vested with the habit by S. Francis in person, and was appointed first Provincial Minister of the March of Ancona. Holding the same office in after years in the East, he died, in the year 1282 at an advanced age. His companion witness, Fr. Rayneri joined the Brotherhood in the middle of the century and died on Nov. 1st, 1304. Fr. Massaeus of Marignano, the authority of the abovementioned Friars, and whom they purport to quote, was the life-long friend and trusted spiritual adviser of S. Francis. The year of his death is not known. The internal evidence of the document leaves unprejudiced minds with little doubt of its authenticity; and P. Holzapfel's conclusions may be accepted: that a consensus of trustworthy contemporary testimony favours the grant of a Plenary Indulgence by Pope Honorius III, to S. Francis, and that the Indulgence was at first not as well-known, or as populary frequented as it undoubtedly became in the latter half of the XIIIth century. The text of the document referred to above, runs as follows :

" Ista est quaedem charta sive strumentum publicum de concessione
" indulgentiae Sanctae Mariae de Angelis facta et concessa per domi-
" num Honorium apud Perusium.

" In nomine Domini amen. Ego Fr. Benedictus de Aretio qui olim
" fui cum beato Francisco cum adhuc viveret et divina gratia operante
" ipse pater sanctissimus ad suum ordinem me recepit, qui sociorum suo-
" rum socius fui et cum ipsis frequenter et in vita sancti patris nostri
" et post ipsius recessum de hoc mundo ad patrem cum eisdem de
" secretis ordinis frequenter collationem habui, confiteor me frequenter
" audisse a quodam supradictorum sociorum beati Francisci qui voca-
" batur fr. Masseus de Marignano, qui fuit homo veritatis et proba-
" tissimae vitae quod ipse fuit cum b. Francisco apud Perusium ante
" praesentiam domini papae Honorii, cum petivit indulgentiam omnium
" peccatorum pro illis qui contriti et confessi convenirent ad locum
" Sanctae Mariae de Angelis, qui alio nomine Portiuncula noncupatur,
" prima die Kalendarum Augusti vespere dictae diei usque ad vesperas
" sequentis diei.

" Quae indulgentia cum fuisset tam humiliter quam constanter a
" beato Francisco postulata, fuit tandem a summo pontifice liberalis-
" sime concessa, quamvis diceret ipse pontifex non esse consuetudinis
" apostolicae sedis talem indulgentiam facere.

" Haec eadem supradicto modo confiteor ego fr. Raynerius de Ma-
" riano de Aretio socius venerabilis fr. Benedicti me audisse frequenter
" a supradicto fratre Masseo socio beati Francisci, cui fratri Masseo
" ego frater Raynerius amicus specialissimus fui.

" Lectae et publicatae supradictae collationes, apud cellam fratris
" Benedicti de Aretio, coram fratre Compagno de Burgo, coram fratre
" Caro de Aretio, fratre Raynaldo de Castellione, fratre Homodeo de
" Aretio, fratre Aldobrandino de Florentia, fratre Iacobo de Floren-
" tia, fratre Theobaldo de Aretio, fratre Bonaventura de Aretio et
" Massario de Aretio ad haec vocatis et rogatis. In anno Domini
" MCCLXXVII, nemine imperante, papa in ecclesia romana vacante.
" Indictione quinta die dominico ultimo Octobris. Ego Johannes no-
" tarius filius olim.... praedictis omnibus interfui, et de mandato vene-
" rabilis fratris Benedicti et fratris Raynerii scripsi et publicavi ".

(27) P. Holzapfel's suggestion to date Olivi's treatise about the year
1280, the object of the Friars audience being to obtain the papal
sanction for their General's decree, " hoc propter cupiditatis notam,
qua posset ab invidis falsa vel minus sacra indulgentia publicari et
divotio minorari », lends added interest to " An Ensample of exceeding piety and holiness ".

(28) ' Divina Commedia ', Cary's translation (pp. 93 et seq.) "Those
who have been guilty of simony.... are fixed with the head down-
wards in certain apertures, so that no more than the legs appear
with out, and on the soles of their feet are seen burning flames. Dante
is taken down by Virgil into the bottom of the gulf and there finds
Pope Nicholas III, whose evil deeds together with those of other
Pontiffs are badly reprehended ". Cf. the entire Canto XIX, and especially the lines 68-77.

> What then of me requirest? If to know
> So much imports thee, who I am, that thou
> Hast therefore down the bank descended, learn
> That in the mighty mantle I was robed,
> And of a she-bear was indeed the son,
> So eager to advance my whelps, that there
> My having in my purse above I stow'd,
> And here myself. Under my head are dragged
> The rest, my predecessors in the guilt
> Of simony.....

(29) Cf. G. VILLANI, ' Cronica ', Lib. 7, Caps LIV and LVIII, " In the year afore-said (1277), Messer Gian Guatani Cardinal, of the house of Orsini, was elected Pope ; which he being yet in minor orders and a cardinal, led a full honest and virtuous life, t'is said in sooth that he had kept the flower of his mandood. But having become Pope he shewed a masterful spirit entertaining mighty enterprises for love of his kinsfolk, labouring steadfastly for their profit and advancement. And thus was he the first or nearly so in whose court open simony was practised for his family, whereby the Pope advanced them greatly in lands and castles and in gifts of money beyond all the other Romans in the brief span of his days. He created seven Cardinals mostly of his own kin.... and he erected amidst other mighty works the noble palaces of the Popes by S. Peters.... " Nothing now remains of this Pontiff's magnificent projects, for which a long pontificate would scarce have sufficed ; even his tomb in old S. Peters having been destroyed in the rebuilding of the Basilica two centuries later. " In the year 1281 in the month of August Pope Nicholas of the Orsini departed this life in the city of Viterbo ". " Nicholas III, though of robust complexion, sober habit of life and in seeming enjoyment of good health, little knew that three short years were to represent the span of his reign. He had gone to spend the summer months at Soriano, near Viterbo, where overtaken by a stroke which deprived him of speech ; he expired upon a date variously stated by different authorities between August 22d and September 1st, 1280 ". (Cf. ' Storia dei Papi ', Vol. 10. Bianchi-Giovini, Turin, 1883).

(30) " On Nov 30 th, 1277, the Cardinal-Deacon Giovanni Gaetano Orsini was elected to the Pontificate, by the Conclave assembled at Viterbo, under the name of Nicholas III, from his titular church of S. Niccolò al Carcere. Said to have been the handsomest Prelate of his day, Cardinal Orsini was surnamed " il Composto " from the dignity of his bearing, reserved manner and polished speech. Prudent and adroit in counsel, he enjoyed a high reputation for ability in the frequent Conclaves that followed in rapid succession in the two years prior to his own election.

(31) The Cistercian Order, an offshoot of the Benedictines, founded by S. Bernard of Clairvaux (1090-1153).

(32) " S. Paul's Epistle to the Corinthians ", II, v, 8.

(33) Name spelled Rodori in the Padua MS., perhaps Ciudad-Rodrigo ?

The proclamation of the Porziuncula Indulgence. (Tiberio d'Assisi).

(34) The first or old church of Santa Croce was already in existence in 1228. A Bull issued by Pope Innocent IV, at Perugia in 1252 granted an Indulgence of 40 days to all those who by alms and good works should contribute to the work of building the new great church of the Franciscans the splendour of which was to rival Assisi itself. In the year 1295, the Comune of Florence decreed a monthly payment of 200 lesser florins for one year from the mont of April, " in hedifitio et pro hedifitio et opere ecclesie Fratrum Minorum de Florentia utinam feliciter secundum formam statuti initiando et faciendo....". Legacies had already poured in for the purpose, and we learn from Villani (Lib. VIII, Cap. 7.), that in the year of Christ 1294, on the day of the Holy Cross of May.... many bishops, prelates, priests, and religious, with the Podestà and the Captain, and the Priors and all the good folk of Florencemen and women attended the blessing of the stones of the foundations thereof with great state and circumstance ".

(35) This Ensample recurs also in the " Speculum Vitae B. Francisci of Frate Fabiano Ungaro ".

(36) Assisi. It should be noted here that the original mediaeval Italian spelling has been adhered to throughout.

(37) Repeated with variants in the Legenda Maior of S. Bonaventure, where the Spanish noblemans birthplace is called Ylerda. Lerida ?

(38) ' Gospel after S. Luke. Ch. X. v. 7-8 '.. eating and drinking such things : for the labourer is worthy of his hire.... And into whatsoever city ye enter, and they receive you, eat such things as are set before you.

(39) Cf. ' Series Provinciarum Ord. FF. Min.; P. H. GOLUBOVICH, O. F. M. in ' Arch. Fran. Hist." Ann. I, fasc. I, p. 5-6). Anno 1223. - Instituitur Prov. Angliae vivente adhuc S. Francisco. Angliae Prov. Huius primus Minister fuit Fr. Agnellus de Pisis " qui a b. Francisco in proximo capitulo generali (scil. an. 1223) destinatus est provincialis Minieter in Angliam ", quam cum sociis ingressus est anno sequenti, scil. 1224.

(40) Canturia Canterbury, spelled Carturia in the Padua MS.

(41) In the Padua MS. the Porter and not the young Monk carries refreshment to the unwelcome guests in the shape of beer " zervosa ", instead of wine. An Italian origin for the Riccardian text of the Legend, would be inferred from this variant.

(42) ABINGDON. The Monastery of Abingdon was surrendered at the Reformation in 1538, and a Grammar-School founded in 1563. The name is spelled *Window* in the Padua MS. suggesting the New